MW00982110

ALASKA BOUND

and Gagged

By: **Joei Carlton Hossack**

Skeena Press
PMB 9385
P.O. Box 2428
Pensacola, Florida
32513
SkeenaPress@Hotmail.com

Published by: Skeena Press
                  PMB 9385,
                  P.O. Box 2428,
                  Pensacola, Florida 32513

Copyright © 2003   Joei Carlton Hossack

Editors: Joei Carlton Hossack & Elizabeth Mittler

Cover Design: Ralph Roberts
                     Alexander Books
                     A Division of Creativity Inc.

ISBN Number: 0-9657509-4-9

Library of Congress Number: Applied For

Printed in the United States of America
Printing: 10 9 8 7 6 5 4 3 2

Dedication Page

To my family and friends who welcome me whenever I show up on their doorstep.

To my nieces, Rena and Rhonda, who bring laughter into my life.

Books by the same author:

Restless From The Start
ISBN Number: 0-9657509-0-6
Library of Congress Number: 97-91654
$10.95 U.S.   Available: Amazon.Com

Everyone's Dream Everyone's Nightmare
ISBN Number   0-9657509-1-4
Library of Congress Number: 98-90573
$13.95 U.S.   Available: Amazon.Com
or through distributor Alexander Books: 1-800-472-0438
E-Books: Booksforpleasure.com

Kiss This Florida, I'm Outta Here
ISBN Number   0-9657509-2-2
Library of Congress Number: 00-090236
$13.95 U.S.   Available: Amazon.com
or through distributor Alexander Books: 1-800-472-0438
E-Books: Booksforpleasure.com

A Million Miles From Home
ISBN Number   0-9657509-3-0
Library of Congress Number: 2001 126663
$13.95 U.S.   Available: Amazon.com
or through distributor Alexander Books: 1-800-472-0438
E-Books: Booksforpleasure.com

ALASKA BOUND
and Gagged

OR

How I drove from Sarasota, Florida to Alaska in only six and a half months, spending more money than my yearly salary, ruining my camper and having seven major vehicle breakdowns……... but only ONE mental breakdown.

Chapter One

In The Beginning There Was This Crazy Person

No, I don't understand about your wanting to "get out of there." It sounds to me like you enjoy the country fairs, being a docent at the opera, teaching knitting and weaving, computer classes, dinner and dancing with your friends and the comfort of your own home. Why do you want to "schlep" ten thousand miles driving alone in your van hoping to see moose or a Kodiak bear on a floating iceberg in the Bering Sea. I'm not worried about your capabilities and independence because you don't want me to be concerned, but...... So wrote my sister in a letter dated March 30, 1995.

"Mona" I answered, "if that bear is single, he's in trouble."

*   *   *   *   *

I could never understand why most people seem to be so content with their status quo while others, like myself, feel a certain urgency to roam the earth looking for what....excitement, adventure, trouble.....what?

Perhaps my sister was right. Why couldn't I just stay home and let trouble find me for a change? But to be honest it was much too late for that option. I was already in a routine that did not include sitting around and waiting for a "life" to fall into my lap or for some hundred and two year old Prince

1

Charming to knock on my door looking for a younger woman who would drive him from doctor to doctor until his cataract surgery.

Winters found me stuck in Sarasota, Florida looking for "trouble" that I never did find, I'm sorry to say. Summers, on the other hand, found me trotting around the globe in search of excitement. This summer would be no exception.

I still cannot believe that I purchased a motorhome, stocked it with food, fuel and propane and acquired enough knowledge to fill a thimble almost to the brim and took off for adventure.....or trouble, as I prefer to think of it. Boy did I find it on this trip.

I left Sarasota driving a friend's van sometime around the middle of April. Jackie wanted her van in New Jersey and I had to get to Canada, loaded down with all kinds of personal possessions, kitchen wares and camping equipment but without my own vehicle, an emerald green, 1993 Ford Escort wagon. I wanted to purchase the motorhome in Canada.

It took me no time at all to adjust to driving the brown, limited edition Toyota and since Jackie had just had it serviced from stem to stern I was not anticipating any mechanical problems. The drive from Florida to Montreal was as tedious as it had always been. Fortunately just before she handed over the keys I suggested that she give me a letter stating that she had loaned me the vehicle and that I had her permission to take it into Canada.

At the border I was asked the usual questions. "Where do you live?"

"Sarasota, Florida."

"Where are you heading?"

"Montreal."

"Why are you driving a vehicle with New Jersey plates?"

"I have this letter," I started to explain and reached over for my purse.

"Pull over, park and go inside the office," was the next recommendation.

That I did. I showed the permission letter to the officer inside, who checked it over very carefully, before returning it and coming outside to check the van.

It was inspected from the glove compartment to the storage bay. The boxes with used pots and pans, plastic dishes and cups and cutlery were opened and inspected. My sleeping bag was laid out flat and the pillows removed from their cases. The large, black plastic bag containing my clothes was emptied and each garment squeezed and then turned inside out. Another bag containing face cloths, washcloths, dishcloths and towels was also turned upside down and scanned. When he was satisfied that I was bringing nothing unsavory into the country I was "invited" into the office. My name was registered in the computer and after checking the official signed, sworn and dated letter from Jackie they saw no reason to detain me further.

I spent a half hour in their parking lot putting everything back in their bags or boxes so they would not roll around the back of the van. I breathed a sigh of relief when I was finally back on my way. It was a mere forty-mile drive to my brother's house in Montreal.

Chapter Two

The Hunt is On

The quest for a Volkswagen Westphalia, my vehicle of choice although I have no idea why, started immediately. I picked up copies of the *Buy and Sell for Boats and Recreational Vehicles* and another *Buy and Sell for Cars and Trucks* with a couple of pages at the back of the magazine devoted to motorhomes and began my search in earnest. I wanted nothing older than five years old. It had to be rust free and preferable rustproof. A little scratch or two was okay but no major dents or dings. I needed low mileage so I could add thousands to the odometer on my pilgrimage. When nothing showed up in that latest issue of the magazine or in the newspapers I started hunting down dealers. There seemed to be nothing in a recent vintage in the immediate vicinity that looked interesting. There were a few in northern Quebec.

I decided that before I traveled the hundreds of miles into the hinterland of Jonquire and Chicoutimi, so far north from Montreal that I would need a team of dogs, a sled and a long enough extension cord to plug in my electric blanket, I would check out availability in Toronto. At least there I spoke the language and had friends I could stay with during my search.

In Toronto I found my perfect toy. Everything on my mental list, and a few extras that were not on my list, checked out. It was dark metallic blue in color without a scratch on it. It was stick shift with a full alarm system installed and a bicycle rack that hung on the back door. There was a portipotty hidden under a padded box seat. It had four extra tires, not on rims. There was a giant puke-green tote to be used as a gray water tank extender. There were bits and pieces that didn't look like anything I had seen before and I never did figure out what they were used for.

The owners had purchased it new in Germany and had traveled extensively in Europe. It had less than twenty thousand miles on it and since the couple needed the money for fertility drug therapy they were anxious to get rid of it. I could afford what they were asking. I left a down payment and promised to pick it up the following week. I drove Jackie's van back to Montreal. The following week I was a passenger in Joan and Cary Dressler's car. They were headed for Toronto and the wedding of a nephew. I delivered a cashier's check and picked up my new motorhome. I drove it back to Montreal. With a couple of days rest I drove Jackie's Toyota, with one stop in New Hampshire to visit my nephew Robert and his wife Laura, back to New Jersey. Jackie drove me to Amy and Norman Prestup's house in North Arlington, New Jersey for a couple of days to visit with friends and discuss my travel plans. Two days later the Prestups put me on a bus to Montreal where my niece Rena, despite the fact that I was over three hours late, was waiting for me.

In the one month since I had left Florida I had driven or been a passenger in a moving vehicle a total of four thousand five hundred miles and had not been anywhere yet.

While in Montreal I contacted the Westphalia club and decided to stay close to home until I could get some pointers on how all the incidentals worked. The group was having a rally in May. I was invited to join them. It would be three days of getting together with like-minded people. I looked forward to it.

Chapter Three

An Easy Add-A-Room

I arrived at the campground in Adolphustown, halfway between Montreal and Toronto, so loaded with incidentals that there was not much room for me. I searched out Richard and Beverley Hood. Beverley was the one I had spoken to over the phone and Richard was the president of the club. That night around the campfire I told the group that I would be driving to Alaska. I mentioned it only in passing since I was not really feeling like part of the group. I was required to join the club; my name would be on the roster but would not be at any of the future camp-outs. Not another word was mentioned about my trip.

I listened to stories about their last camp-out and secretly wished that I had a companion to go to Alaska with, as long as I felt I had to go at all. They seemed to have so many stories about all the fun that they had as a group.

The next day was bright and warm and I dragged all the extras out onto the grass. I opened the large box marked add-a-room just to see what it was. It didn't take long for the whole group to come around and inspect. The directions, written in English, French, Spanish and a couple of Oriental languages, didn't come close to explaining how this thing was supposed to be set up or attached to the side of the motorhome. Four guys took a side each and pulled. Beverley directed while another able-bodied male walked around seeing where things were supposed to go. There were unattached poles that had to be inserted somewhere. There were extra lengths of canvas that had to be wrapped around something. There were nuts and bolts that had to connect things. One hour and forty-five minutes, five diligent workers and one instructor later I decided that it wasn't worth the effort and I would not take the tent with me. I didn't think I would be sitting still long enough in any one spot to need it. In addition to the other problems it would not stand on it's own four tent poles.

When Richard saw all the junk that surrounded my van he offered a corner of his garage to be used as storage. I thanked him for his offer, took his address and we made arrangements for me to follow him back to their home in Whitby, Ontario about forty miles east of Toronto.

The weekend was relaxing with lots of activities planned. As a group we managed to tour the rolling green countryside stopping for a picnic lunch in a park at the water's edge. We watched families flying giant kites and kids checking out the water pools for any signs of life. We toured a cheese factory, enjoying some warm cheese curds, and stopped at a bakery to purchased fresh bread and buns for our morning coffee on our way back to the campground. There was one older man that was unaccompanied. Although they insisted we all go in our own vehicle so we could look like a force of giant bugs crawling across the surface of the earth I rode with Lawrie, the other solo, and left my VW in the campground. No one seemed to mind. We had a potluck supper and ended each night sitting around the campfire swapping stories. I remained remarkable shy.

The group was helpful in pointing out little hidden compartments, that I never would have found, and where to use little plastic boxes to store bits and pieces. They showed me how to pack and where to put items I wouldn't need all the time.

Although they were pleasant, almost nothing was said about my upcoming trip. I know that they felt it was too long a journey for a woman to be traveling alone and that in the end I probably wouldn't go. They obviously didn't know me well, if at all. They had no way of knowing that guts, determination, spunk and lunacy ran in my family and whatever I set out to do I usually did.

Before leaving most of the group came over to wish me well. I followed the Hoods back to their home and spent a wonderful evening getting to know them. They picked up a couple of pizzas and I purchased a bottle of Greek wine for dinner. Their son Christopher joined us for the pizza. Since both their daughters were away I had a bedroom to myself.

The following morning Richard and I went through my van deciding what to keep and what to leave. The four spare tires without rims, the puke-green tote on wheels, the add-a-room tent all stayed behind. I had my late husband's tool kit with me. It was so heavy that I needed two hands to lift it. Richard went through the blue metal box.

"If you need this many tools to fix something," he said, "you won't be able to fix it yourself."

He left me with a couple of different shapes of screwdrivers, a wrench set, a siphon, black hockey tape and other bits and pieces that I might need. The rest he put in a bag and hoisted that and all the other rejects up to the rafters of his garage. I immediately felt lighter and so did my van.

We spent the day picking up travel maps and guidebooks at the Canadian Automobile Association, groceries at the supermarket for a spaghetti dinner and another bottle of wine. We spent the evening talking, laughing and checking out the map for the route I would take and the guidebooks for things

I didn't want to miss along the way. It was the last night I spent in absolute comfort.

I returned to Toronto. I had the van serviced at a Volkswagen dealer who gave it a spotlessly clean bill of health. I purchased a pressure cooker, a frying pan, and one small saucepan. I loaded up with paper goods. I packed the cupboards with can goods and the refrigerator with perishables and took off heading north.

I stopped to say hello and goodbye to my friend Pat Thomas living in Beeton, Ontario. It was raining. The weather was supposed to turn nasty for the next few days. She invited me to stay. I stayed three days. I left in sunshine.

I stopped in Bradford, Ontario. I had left about seventy-five hand-knit sweaters at a small shop and hoped to pick up some money from the sale. I was greeted with a hug and a smile from Helen and served tea and homemade scones. With the niceties out of the way I asked about the sweater sales.

"People were trying to bargain with me. I didn't want to let them go so cheap," she said. "I put them away over a year ago and never brought them out again."

She literally knocked the wind out of me with this new revelation. I packed up the five huge black garbage bags filled with my hand-knits. There was no corner to stuff them in so I just piled them up on the floor. I was off.....in more ways than one.

Since my first day on the road had already stated with a bang, a couple of thuds and a giant bust I just wanted to make it to the border so I could feel sure that I was really on my way. I hadn't even driven fifty miles when the rain started. I spent the rest of that day rather uncomfortably traveling slowly in and out of cloudbursts.

Crossing the border into the United States was a bit of a nuisance. The border guard seemed suspicious and glared at me without saying a word for much too long. When he finally did speak there was not the slightest hint of friendliness in this voice. I'm not sure if he wanted to intimidate me because I was a woman or because I was traveling alone or because my vehicle was loaded to the hilt even though he couldn't really see inside from where he was standing. Since my passport and paperwork were in order he didn't annoy me for long. I was glad to be moving on. I headed north.

I had gone as far as I wanted to for my first day. I stopped at Lakeport State Park just north of the Port Huron border crossing. I was in Michigan. It was four-thirty in the afternoon.

Chapter Four

Nobody's Little Girlfriend

The first days and nights of any trip for me were tough and this one proved to be no exception even though the first minutes after arrival were busy ones. I made sure I was on reasonably level ground, having to back it up and bring it forward a few times before managing it. I raised the top of the camper, opened a few windows to get some fresh air in, put my deck chair outside leaning against the van and checked the refrigerator for what might look appealing for dinner. Since I wasn't hungry I didn't see much that looked appetizing.

I hoisted my bicycle off the rack and went for a ride around the campground. The path was paved and no one else seemed to be using it for walking or riding. There were very few campers in the park. The few hardy souls that were there, myself included, seemed to have congregated around the washrooms and showers. There was no one to talk to in the outlying reaches of the campground. I was disappointed. After a few spins around the outer reaches of the park I returned to my site.

To busy myself I prepared a beef stew with carrots, potatoes, mushrooms, celery and a healthy pinch of herbes de Provence, parsley, black pepper and hot sauce. I lit the fire under by new pressure cooker, brought it up to pressure and reduced the heat. While it simmered so did I.

I opened my deck chair, took a Ken Follett novel out of a bag of about ten recently acquired books, propped my feet up inside my van, and relaxed while dinner cooked. As hard as I tried I couldn't concentrate.

Although there were few people in the campground visitors started to arrive in cars, on motorcycles and in trucks greeting my neighbors in cheery tones, to the point where I wanted to slap them and send them home. They didn't look like they came prepared to spend the night. They were just there for the evening, tormenting me without even looking my way.

I checked on dinner. I added some flour and water to my stew. It didn't take long to thicken up. I scooped out a couple of ladles full and ate with the bowl on my lap while reading. I could feel the depression that was about to consume me. I ate quickly. I went into the camper to wash the dishes and when I went back outdoors to finish the chapter in my book, the elder in the group of neighbors invited to join them. I was delighted. I put my book in the camper, closed the door to keep the flying bugs out, picked up my chair and ambled over to their campfire. I introduced myself to the group of about fifteen adults and way too many children for my liking and only a couple of the women introduced themselves back.

When one of the men asked if I was traveling alone. I answered "yes."

The same guy asked where I was headed and I answered "Alaska" and that basically stopped all conversation. The group was momentarily struck dumb. They went back to conversing with their friends and relatives and I moved my chair closer to the fire thinking it was just a lull in the conversation. I wasn't included in any of the conversation that seemed to be very personal and unfamiliar. I suddenly had the feeling that I was intruding and I hadn't been there long enough to feel comfortable about leaving and going back to my camper to read or watch television. I sat like a lump saying nothing.

ALASKA BOUND *and Gagged*

As the darkness engulfed us and the air became heavy with cold moisture, the group started to disperse. The couples with small children picked up the toys that were scattered around, packed up their car, and went home. The older ones feeling the chill, wrapped themselves in sweaters and went back to their campers or left in a truck. The guy on the motorcycle left. The wife of the old guy left the campsite to sit at a neighbor's campfire. The old guy, an even older friend of his and myself sat by the fire. When I got up to leave the old man asked me to stay.

When his friend left I was trapped. I couldn't go without hurting his feeling since he obviously still wanted to talk. He explained that this was to be the gathering of his friends and family. His massively overweight body was filled with fluid and with cancer. The chemotherapy hadn't worked. He could hardly walk. Breathing was an effort. Talking was almost impossible. I sat and listened.

When he asked why I was traveling alone I told him it had been a dream of my husbands to see Alaska. I was fulfilling his dream. It was just about the time I started talking that Jim's wife returned. She patted him on the shoulder.

"You're going to have to leave your little girlfriend now and come inside," she leaned over and whispered into his ear.

If she thought only her husband heard this comment she was sadly mistaken. I guess the old broad learned to whisper in a sawmill.

"I'm talking to my friend," he said, "I'll be in shortly."

"Leave your little girlfriend NOW and come inside," she repeated giving me an icy hard stare.

My heart shriveled.

We never did get back to talking about anything of interest and I wanted to run as far and as fast as I could. I excused myself. I needed to get back to the security of my little home. I was close to tears when I got up. I fumbled with my chair, folded it up and went back to the van. Except for the border guard these were the first people I had spoken to all day. I took down the sheets, blankets and arranged the pillows already on my bed. I turned on my black-and-white television set and allowed it to drone on in the background not knowing or caring what was playing. I crawled into bed and allowed the tears to come hoping for exhaustion and sleep. My mind worked overtime.

I had lost a beautiful, fifty-two year old husband to a heart attack, so naturally I wanted to run off with a seventy year old, three hundred pound man suffering from cancer. "How could I resist?" I hissed the words sarcastically under my breath. "Little girlfriend indeed," suddenly feeling the daggers of anger before the next crying jag hit.

The next morning everyone milled around outside at the adjacent camping spot. While they busied themselves with breakfast I cleaned up, packed up and left without saying a world to anyone. No one even looked my way as I pulled out.

I spent much of the day contemplating the events of the previous day. I cried a bit because I was sure that this sort of pettiness would plague me, to various degrees, all the way to Alaska and back. When I wasn't feeling sorry for myself I was laughing at the fact that as a fifty year old, gray-haired and thirty pounds overweight woman, the old hag considered me a vamp that would run off with her man.

The more I thought about it the more I had to chuckle. It had been eons since I had been looked upon as a femme fatale. Thirty men to every woman in Alaska I had heard on the Oprah Show before leaving Sarasota.

Look out world!

Chapter Five

Panic

With nothing to compare them to, each of these early days would produce some new challenges, a few delightful experiences and far too many worrisome fears. I stopped that morning in a supermarket parking lot. So I wouldn't feel like I was abusing the privilege, I picked up a few necessities in the store and after putting the items away, I had a bowl of cold cereal for breakfast and looked over the maps while still in their lot. I decided on a slow trip north on what was called the Lake Huron Circle Tour.

This was cottage country. It had the sweet-smelling air of freshly mowed grass. It had wide-open spaces and when cars or trucks passed they did it at a reasonable speed. Only the occasional idiot passed on the inside, soft-shoulder lane and blew up a mini dust storm as he flew by. At Bad Axe I stopped and took a picture of the town sign. Although the picture showed a broken axe handle no one seemed to know the story that went along with the name. I drove on to Sanilac State Historic Park. It was only thirteen miles south. According to my guidebook the park contained one thousand-year old Sanilac Petroglyphs, American Indian rock carvings consisting of figures that resembled animals, birds and humans etched on sandstone. I was anxious to see them.

I arrived early afternoon and pulled into the nearly empty parking lot. There was one other motorhome and their door was open. I parked my camper and went to talk to the middle-aged couple whom I happen to disturb having lunch. I apologized for the intrusion and, with a friendly smile, was invited in to join them for coffee. While they finished their lunch they told me about the petroglyphs and how well worth the walk it was.

"It's only about a half mile up the dirt path," said Marty, "but since it's closed today you'll have to climb over the fence. Don't worry," he said, "it's easy to do and you'll start seeing the etchings as soon as you enter."

I thanked them for the information and coffee and went back to my camper for some lunch before the trek. I was munching on a bagel and butter when Marty and June came by my camper to say goodbye. They wished me well on my journey and I watched as they pulled out of the parking lot.

I could feel my heart beating in my throat as their motorhome rounded the corner and went out of my sight. My lunch was suddenly dry and I couldn't swallow it. My breaths were coming in short gasps. I took a couple sips of my drink but it didn't help much. A primal fear suddenly seized me, paralyzing me. I looked out into the parking lot and saw nothing. Certainly nothing that would produce the panic that I was feeling. I was alone in the parking lot. I would be alone on the trail. For a split second I wondered if someone was watching, waiting for me to make a wrong move. Waiting for me to step out of my camper. Waiting for me just over the hill on the deserted trail. I threw my lunch into the refrigerator. I locked all the doors with one button on the door panel. I jumped into the driver's seat, fumbled with the key until it was in the ignition switch and took off hoping that I was heading back towards town. My heart was pounding so hard it hurt my ears. I had absolutely no control. I fought back waves of nausea. I was in the midst of a full-blown panic attack.

ALASKA BOUND *and Gagged*

As soon as I reached the next town and saw people milling about I felt better. I didn't stop. I drove to Frankenmuth not seeing or enjoying much along the way. I wanted to stop early and recover from whatever it was that happened to me.

The campground, walking distance from Bronner's Christmas Store, was twenty-eight dollars per night which I chose not to afford. I asked if there was something a little cheaper in the vicinity and was directed to a campground in a churchyard on the other side of town. Since all roads lead to Bronner's there was not much chance of getting lost in town. I eventually found my way.

I pulled in and discovered that there was only one other camper and it looked deserted. I set up my camper but I was not going to commit myself to staying until I met the other people. After an uncomfortable experience I wanted a relaxing evening and night. If necessary I would pay the twenty-eight bucks but only if it was absolutely necessary.

Harold and Joanne Genert returned late in the afternoon. They waved an enthusiastic greeting and called me over for a glass of wine. I brought my own wineglass. We wined. We dined, sharing what we each had available. We talked until way past dark and the bugs made their presence pointedly known. I asked how comfortable they were in an empty campground and was told that their entire camping club with about fifty members had left that morning. They were staying another couple of days to "catch their breath" after a hectic few days. I decided to stay a couple of days as well. According to my guidebook there was much to see, do and eat.

Frankenmuth is an historical little Bavarian village dating back to 1845 with a different theme for each tourist shop in town.....a clock maker, a wood carver, a candle maker, a baker making bread visible through the window and the ever popular homemade ice cream shop. Popular with me anyway. Frankenmuth meaning "courage of the Franconians" was settled by fifteen Franconians sent by the pastors in Bavaria who were concerned over the religious life of Lutheran immigrants and their American Indian neighbors. The Indian tribe moved away but the Bavarian heritage remained and was reinforced by other arrivals from Germany.

The thirty-five bell automatic carillon in the Bavarian Inn's Glockenspiel Tower plays selected melodies followed by a presentation of carved wooden figures depicting the legend of the Pied Piper of Hamelin. Nearby was a wooden covered bridge that spanned the Cass River.

I spent the morning walking around town but the afternoon was devoted to Bronner's Christmas Wonderland. The store is open three hundred sixty-one days a year, is the size of four football fields and boasts over fifty thousand trims and gifts. Everywhere I looked something was dazzling or sparkling or swinging and swaying. They showed a movie and had historical information available. I purchased a little angel to hang over my visor and protect me (from my own panic attacks no doubt).

Back at the campground, we compared notes on how the day had gone. While I shopped, my friends toured the outlying area by car. Of course they had already been to town and had spent a number of hours at Bronner's.

Before parting the next morning, we each took the time to give our vehicles a thorough washing inside and out. We said our good byes and headed off in opposite directions.

Chapter Six

A Chance Meeting with a Fugitive

I headed north past Saginaw with my own rendition of Lefty Frizzell's song rattling around in my brain. Not knowing many of the words I repeatedly started with "I was born in Saginaw, Michigan" and ended up humming the rest of the tune for the next five hours.

I stopped at a gas station in Au Gres, checked the local phone book and called the home of Denny and Martie Erikson, acquaintances from my winter home, that now seemed about as remote as the place I was heading to. Although Denny would have preferred spending twelve months a year in Sarasota, Martie wanted no part of Florida's overwhelming heat and humidity. She insisted that they keep their summer home overlooking Lake Huron. Denny and Martie were my Friday night companions at a local hangout that served a mountain of all-you-can-eat oysters on the half-shell and somewhat tasty chicken wings along with watered-down two-for-the-price-of-one drinks. Our Friday nights were a tradition until they put my picture up on the wall with a red circle around it and a slash mark through it. When that didn't keep me out of the place they took oysters off the all-you-can-eat menu and there wasn't much point in going just for the mediocre chicken wings. I'm sure their profit margin rose dramatically when I was no longer heaping a dozen or more oysters on my plate and going back five or six times for refills with Denny nipping at my heels to see if he could better me. He never won.

Martie was home and seemed delighted to hear from me. She directed me to a country store on the main road and was waiting for me when I arrived. I followed her home. Denny was out.

Their home was lovely with comfortable, overstuffed couches, chairs and a love seat in printed greens, pink and burgundy. The dining room furniture and kitchen table and chairs were solid wood and all the cabinets were built-in. The house was neat but evidence of being well lived in and enjoyed was everywhere. Martie loved needlepoints and handmade quilts. She had unfinished handwork or a half-read book at almost every chair. Denny's golf clubs were in the one corner. The rooms facing the water had enormous picture windows and we had lunch and talked for a couple of hours in full view of the lake. I waited as long as I could to say hello to Denny but I didn't want to drive in the dark so I left around three in the afternoon not knowing where the next open campground would be.

Within the hour, about thirty to forty miles up the road, I arrived at Tawas Point State Park and decided to stay. I set up the camper, did a little biking and returned before dark to decide what I would have for dinner.

I was not too thrilled when I discovered that I was parked shoulder-to-shoulder with a fugitive. He was introduced as Cooper. He was young and naturally blond with soft brown eyes and long eyelashes. He seemed so friendly that I could not have imagined what dirty deed had put him behind bars.

Cooper's caretakers, an older couple, kept him on a short leash. The drama in real life story was spewed out when I put my hand out to shake his.....paw, that he gave me freely. Cooper was a gorgeous six-year-old golden retriever. He was certainly friendly when I knelt down to stroke his fur. Within seconds he had rolled over onto his back and allowed me to scratch his belly.

"I can't imagine him being a fugitive," I said.

"Well," said his owner, "twern't his fault. Twelve-year-old brat down the road kept teasing 'im. Cooper finally had 'nough, jumped on him and scratched his shoulder. Kid's mother called the police. Cooper was arrested. Got to keep 'im tied up now."

"Why doesn't mother keep the kid tied up? Sounds like that's who needs tying." I said still scratching Cooper's tummy.

"Yup, you're sure right," he answered.

By the time I was through playing with the dog, my stomach was growling and wanted attention. I went into the camper and closed the door since the mayflies seemed to be swarming and I didn't want them in my camper. They looked like mosquitoes but didn't bite. They didn't have to. They were still disgusting.

I was up and out early the next morning. I invited Cooper to come along on a walk with me to the lighthouse but the owners didn't want to risk it. I wondered if it was the same three strikes and your out for dogs as well as humans. I didn't think to ask and went on my way for the relatively short walk to the lighthouse. The walk was paved to the edge of the tall-grass area and then it was a wide, well-tromped path. I had to step over some large, wooden signs and a few posts that were scattered about, but nothing stopped me. Other than the lighthouse that was not occupied or working, there didn't seem to be much of interest on the point so I turned around and walked back. Before stepping over the signs and posts I picked up one of them and discovered in big, black, bold lettering "No Trespassing – Property of Coast Guard" on the other side.

Joei Carlton Hossack

If this book ends abruptly I've been taken out by friendly fire. Until that happens, let me continue.

Chapter Seven

A Fortunate Mistake

The day passed relatively quietly. I visited the museum in Alpena. They featured a presentation called World War II Remembered. Since I had already visited the Normandy Beaches in France, the Jesse Besser Museum was an interesting place to stop. In Rogers City I stopped briefly at the largest open limestone quarry in North America. I spent that night in the Cheboygan State Park.

I was surprised to read in my guidebook that Mackinaw City, anchor of the southern end of the Mackinac Bridge, was a trading post established by the early French settlers around seventeen fifteen. The town now looked like it was built, completed and settled twenty minutes before I arrived. Everything appeared brand spanking new and hotels, both high-rise and strip, were in various stages of completion all along the route. I arrived in time for the annual Soap Opera Fan Fare weekend. Massive tents were set up on the dock and people lined up around and around the parking lot hoping to get a glimpse of or to speak to their favorite star. Since I had never seen a soap opera I felt no urge to stand in line. I wouldn't recognize any one of them if they came up and bit me. Although I think I would be tempted to ask for an autograph on the bottom of a check that included a large bunch of zeros after a six or seven figure, if one of them actually did come up and bite me.

I checked out all the little shops on the main avenue. I had a huge container of homemade ice cream. I purchased a hot dog and fries from a street vendor and relished every artery-clogging moment. I steeled myself for the trip over the bridge.

Going over the bridge into the Upper Peninsula was a bit of a scary drive. I kept my eyes looking forward since it was a long, long way down and the wind did have a tendency to batter me about some. I didn't believe the rumors about the young woman driving a Yugo that flew off the bridge in a windstorm. Since I have some recollection of the tin can Yugo, I would prefer to believe that, in a moment of embarrassment, she actually drove it off the bridge, if she did indeed go off the bridge. Just for the record that was not really what I wanted on my mind while I drove across. Nevertheless, I made it without incident.

The drive across the Upper Peninsula, or U.P. as the Yuppers (pronounced Yoopers) prefer to call it, was long and tedious. On the opposite side of the bridge I changed from the Lake Huron to the Lake Michigan Circle Tour. It all looked the same except there were fewer people, fewer homes and fewer towns. There were more people that waved as I drove by and more old folks that sat on their balconies.

The only campground I found was twenty miles out off the beaten path and even then I ended up at the wrong camping spot. Had I gone straight on the road I had turned off onto I would have ended up in Fayette State Park with all the facilities I wanted and needed. Instead I ended up following another car to a campground with pit toilets and no electricity. Despite my error I ended up meeting some terrific people and thoroughly enjoyed my evening.

Zack and Natalie each had two children. Although they had dated for several months this was their first weekend as a blended family. I think they were delighted to have me around as a diversion. We talked and joked. I was included in their barbecued hot dog and hamburger dinner. They supplied the soft drinks and beer. I supplied the wine and the evening ended long after midnight. We all commented on my fortunate mistake and I got a hug from both before heading back to my camper.

I was on the road early the next day and visited the historical site of Fayette where I was supposed to have been camping. Fayette was a well-preserved 1867 town that thrived along with the iron industry for nearly twenty-five years. When the operation ceased in 1891 the site was abandoned. It was a self-guided walking tour through many empty buildings until going through the museum.

It was in a picturesque setting overlooking the bluffs, very reminiscent of the approach to the White Cliffs of Dover, only in miniature.

Since we each received a folder with a description of all the buildings I sat on one of the park benches provided and studied them. It was so relaxing I just stayed and enjoyed a picnic lunch on the grounds.

Chapter Eight

A Port in the Storm

It didn't take long to get lonely on the road. The Bertolis, Frances and George, were my port in the storm. They were friends from Sarasota and had been my neighbors before moving to a golfing resort a few blocks away. When I left Florida they knew that I would be heading to Alaska but had no idea what route I would be taking or when or if I would be passing their door. How could they know.....I certainly didn't.

"Just call when you get close," was George's suggestion.

When I looked at the map in Iron Mountain, Michigan I discovered that I was about fifteen miles from their home in Florence, Wisconsin. I prayed they would be home.

I called from a Dairy Queen on the highway in Florence after I had eaten a quick lunch. The greeting I got over the phone could not have been warmer. Frances gave me brief instructions to a local restaurant on Highway 2 since they were off the main road and George would drive up and meet me. He certainly was a sight for sore eyes when I saw his long, slender figure leaning against his car waiting for me. He waved for me follow, got into his car and directed me halfway down the steep hill and onto their large, flat driveway. Frances was waiting at the door with a freshly baked pie and ushered me into the living room. She served coffee, a little strong for my liking, and a large wedge of apple pie still warm from the oven and topped with a dollop of whipped cream.

We talked the afternoon away, mostly about my travels, how I was making out on the road and where I would be heading next. That evening I was their guest at a family-style restaurant serving huge portions of fried chicken, sweet corn, mashed potatoes with gravy, and a variety of cakes for dessert. The food was delicious. The company was wonderful and for the first time in a long time I just plain relaxed.

That evening I called my sister in California. She, too, was thrilled that I had caught up with some friends and that, at least for the moment, I was safe. We still planned on meeting someplace down the road. I suggested Jackson Hole, Wyoming which would give me about three weeks without rushing and Mona would have time to get her plans underway. We hung up on a very positive note.

I started the next day with a full course, bacon and egg, breakfast and several cups of coffee. Afterwards I luxuriated in a bath, something that I really missed since I was forced to become a shower person. Coffee and pie, mid-morning on the back deck overlooking a forest, somehow lead to lunch.

By the time I got back on the road it was early afternoon. The drive seemed endless. Before I had gone down the road fifty miles I missed my friends and went over each tidbit of conversation in my mind to pass the time.

I stopped for a short walk to stretch my legs through a new forest area on highway 70 and then transferred to highway 8 heading south. I finally found myself in a county campground. It was quiet with not many other campers around. Despite the fact that it was a relatively short drive day, I was thrilled to finally find myself off the road. The deer were everywhere and white trillium carpeted the forest floor.

Chapter Nine

Bzzt.....Bzzt.....Bzzt

Bzzt.....bzzt.....bzzt.

I awoke swatting in so many different directions that I felt like the little girl in *The Exorcist*. There were so many mosquitoes in my van that had they banded together they would have been the size of a cat.....a giant, smirking Cheshire cat.

Bzzt.....bzzt.....bzzt.

Do I swat the ones buzzing in front of my eyes or do I reach up another three inches and try for the dozen or so that are glued to the ceiling eyeing me a like lunch counter with no vacant seats? Oh what the hell, I mumbled under my breath, I have two hands. I swatted, missed the entire circus and they all swarmed me.

Bzzt.....bzzt.....bzzt.

The closest I came to a solution was a free sample of Johnson's Off Skintastic developed, no doubt, by one of the highly advance blood-suckers to fool the human population. They loved it. They started dive bombing me for the recipe.....or even for just a whiff.

Bzzt.....bzzt.....bzzt.

I got out my trusty swatter. I armed myself to do battle.

By six o'clock in the morning my van was littered with tiny dead bodies and thousands had arrived to attend the funeral.

ALASKA BOUND *and Gagged*

I killed one mosquito on my back window drape that left a bloodstain large enough to cause some suspicion. Thank goodness for DNA testing, I thought. I know that it'll prove a suicide from too much rich food rather than a murder.

There is a country and western song by Dave Dudley about "a tombstone every mile" on the same stretch of highway in the North Woods that I had chosen to camp on. I know what killed them. It was the deadly, blood-sucking mosquito and entourage.

There are several states that claim the mosquito as their national bird. Wisconsin is just one of them. They got my vote.

I didn't wait to have breakfast since I feared ingesting a mouthful of fat, red-bellied, winged things that had more of my blood than I did along with my corn flakes. I didn't want to think unkind thoughts since the Bertolis had welcomed me royally to their state but.....I'm outta here.

Bzzt.....bzzt.....bzzt.

I wasn't on the road long when it started to rain. Heavy, constant rains and not much in the way of interesting scenery produced another long day's drive. I had to pull over onto a vacant lot just south of St. Paul, Minnesota because I could no longer see the road signs through the storm and I was at a critical junction with underpasses and overpasses that went in all directions. I looked around and was not comfortable with my surroundings. I don't think I was in a safe part of the town but just as I turned off the motor the hail started. I had to wait it out and hoped that the hailstones wouldn't crack the air vent on the top of my van or any windows. When the hail stopped I proceeded slowly.

I spent that night well south of Minneapolis in LeSeuer, home of William W. Mayo who in 1864 moved to Rochester where he and his sons founded the Mayo Clinic. The Cosgrove family occupied the same house from 1874 to 1920. The

Cosgrove family started the Green Giant Company. Ho! Ho! Ho.! Once again I was just thrilled to death to be off the road. The front area of the campground, a large open field for tents and such was totally devoid of people but after I paid my money and was told to "display my receipt prominently in the front window" I assumed that there would be others in the back lot.

"Oh, are there a lot of campers out back?" I asked.

"No," she responded, "you'll be the only one back there."

I tried not to wrinkle up my nose too badly or in any way give the impression that I thought she was a couple of sandwiches short of a picnic but was she going to forget that the only person camping there had forgotten to pay. Did I really have to "display it prominently?"

I was indeed alone in the back lot that could easily have supported a hundred or so camping vehicles. I pulled in under a tree, plugged in my electricity, took a couple of sausages out of the freezer and two eggs out of the refrigerator and left them to thaw on the counter. I plugged in my television set and prepared myself for a long, lonely evening.

I was delighted when a big motorhome pulled into a spot across from me. I didn't interrupt when they were setting up camp but as soon as they were done I went over to say hello. We sat under their awning enjoying a glass of wine and a few nibblies.

Husband and wife, Richard and Marion were out on a one-week vacation, even though they had all the time in the world to wander. Richard had been retired for several years and Betty, Marion's elderly widowed sister, was along for the ride and not in any particular hurry to get back to an empty home. They lived in St. Paul and enjoyed touring but preferred staying close to home.

By the time I returned to my camper, the sausages were thawed leaving a runny spot beside the sink, the eggs were at room temperature and I was pleasantly tipsy and starving. I had dinner, made my bed, and slept like the dead.

The days and nights were much too long for me. I had left too early in the season. I needed people around me even if it was just in the evening but there were never many around. Although I refused to admit it out loud or do anything about it, I was beginning to resent the massive undertaking. In the endless hours I spent driving I often wondered if I had bitten off more than I could chew.

Chapter Ten

Little House on the Prairie

The next day, although a little overcast, was warm and I enjoyed a long walk through New Ulm. The town was copied from Ulm in West Germany and famous for its Glockenspiel. Unfortunately it wasn't working at the time so just a few people sat in the park staring up at its face hoping a miracle would occur. The sky started looking ominous and as I walked back to the van it started to sprinkle.

By the time I was moving down the two-lane road the heavens opened up and it didn't take long before I discovered that I couldn't see more than a few feet in front of the van. Seeing a farmhouse on the left side of the street I decided that they wouldn't mind if I used their driveway until the storm subsided. The farmhouse turned out to be The Town Hall that wasn't in use at the time.

I discovered that there were definite advantages to driving around like a snail with everything I owned on my back. I made a sandwich for lunch and to take away the chill I made a cup of instant coffee. I waited and watched as the storm blasted through. All the small trees in its path whipped around threatening to snap. When I saw the clearing in the west I got back on the road, driving as fast as I dared.

My next stop was Sleepy Eye, Minnesota. I visited the museum and the granite obelisk in honor of Chief Ish-Tak-Ah-

ALASKA BOUND *and Gagged*

Bah meaning Sleepy Eye. The Sisseton Dakota Chief is buried under the obelisk, located near the Depot Museum. It was a small museum and I went through everything in less than an hour.

I listened to the news as I drove on to my next stop. It seems that while I waited out the storm at the Town Hall, approximately three miles to the east, a tornado touched down in Sleepy Eye. I saw no evidence of it. An angel must have been riding on my shoulder and I felt grateful.

By the time I stopped at Laura Ingalls Wilder's home in Walnut Grove, the rain had stopped and the sky was a cloudless, baby blue. Her *Little House on the Prairie* books made the area famous and everything has remained exactly as she left it. The schoolhouse was tiny and quaint. The desks remained bolted to the floor. At any one time, the room held no more than a dozen students of various ages and grades. A well-used pot-bellied stove sat in the center of the room.

The inside of her house conjured up ancient memories for me. There were so many pieces I admired in her home that resembled items I had in my home when I was a child, mostly kitchenware. It was so hard for me to imagine that things I had, that I believed were just a few years ago, are now antiques. Where the hell did the time go?

Now, of course, I'm proud to say that everything I owned from the good old days have been replaced with blenders and microwaves and pop corners. But let me continue on before I find myself too old and decrepit to remember even what I had for breakfast ten minutes ago. I spent hours wandering.

The last stop of the day was by far the most interesting, Pipestone National Park. Within a two-hundred-and-eighty-three acre tract of land the pipestone quarries are located and the red stone is used by the Indians to make their ceremonial pipes.

Joei Carlton Hossack

According to one legend the quarry site was discovered by Wahegela, an Omaha Indian woman who followed a white bison to the spot where its hooves "turned the rocks red."

The visitor center contained an audiovisual room and a museum that showed in detail the history of the Indian pipes. The tour through the quarry was self-guided and I could enjoy the quarry, the stone profiles, the geological phenomena, Winnewissa Falls, Lake Hiawatha and Leaping Rock at my leisure. I also enjoyed the Indian Cultural Center where I could watch the pipe-making demonstrations done by the local craftsmen.

The campground located right across the street from the park made my decision an easy one. It was the first campground that I had seen that was relatively crowded and I looked forward to meeting and talking to some new people. Unfortunately that was not to be. As soon as the sun went down weather turned cold with an icy breeze that chilled right to the bone. No one poked a nose or anything else out of the camper. Although a bundle of wood could be purchased for a campfire no one wanted to sit outside.

I walked through the store, picked up a chocolate bar, talked to the owners for an hour or so and returned to my van to watch television.

When I left the following morning the campground was as cold and empty as a witch's heart. It didn't take me long to cross over into South Dakota.

Chapter Eleven

South Dakota

The weather was just as cold when I crossed the border into South Dakota. I headed to Brookings. My first stop of the day was McCrory Gardens, part of South Dakota State University, to wander through the rose, herb and rock maze. It was reported that there were ten thousand flowering annuals and two thousand perennials but it was just too cold for most them to show their delicate faces without earmuffs, a scarf and woolly mittens.

University students, bundled up in drab-looking winter attire, lined the walkways on their hands and knees, digging and planting. I did manage a long walk in, around and through the park and, to be fair, the sun made a concerted effort to come out but again, it was just too early in the season for sun and warmth and I was paying the price.

Despite the sparse botanical offering I did enjoy Brookings. I found the South Dakota Art Museum and walked slowly through the Sioux Tribal Art exhibit, paintings by Oscar Howe and Harvey Dunn and lingered over the Marghab linen collection. It was the finest white work I had ever seen.

I took one of the back roads to Mitchell. The recent flooding had caused many of the roads to be washed over. I had to be careful when I drove through some of the washouts fearing a dip in the road at the wrong spot would swallow my vehicle. I was always relieved when the water didn't go past the middle of my wheels as I inched my way through.

I saw barns and silos and homes sitting in the center of what appeared to be a small lake except that the lake hadn't been there the day before the storm. The fences that would normally keep the livestock safe and in their own yards were now prison walls for them and impossible to scale. Herds of animals huddled onto the tiniest of bare patches stood by the fences hoping someone would come rescue them. They were silent. Perhaps they were all cried out.

The weather was starting to warm up a bit. There were a few more people on the road and I decided to find a campground early because I was headed into tourist country, it was the weekend and I feared not finding a place to stay. The campground I chose had the added feature of cable hookup. I needed to do laundry as well so I didn't mind an early end to my drive day. After leveling, attaching and connecting lines, hoses and wires, I loaded up my laundry basket and was at the laundromat before I could change my mind and leave it for later in the weekend. The laundry room was empty and I was back at my camper all cleaned, fluffed and folded and in front of the television set within a couple of hours.

Mitchell itself was the start of something wonderful. I spent the next morning at the Corn Palace. The exterior is Moorish architecture with minarets and kiosks, portions of which are covered with ears of corn but outlined with local grasses and grains. Each year the pictures change and two to three thousand bushels of various shades of corn and grasses are used to redecorate the building inside and out. The interior contains decorative panels designed by Oscar Howe. The outside panels are illuminated at night or so I was told.

After a popcorn, hot dog and candy apple lunch I darted across the street in the rain to the Enchanted World Doll

Museum. While I viewed the over four thousand antique and modern dolls displayed in over four hundred scenes depicting nursery rhymes, fairy tales and life in the eighteenth and nineteenth centuries, another one of the many storms that seemed to plague this trip, raged outside. Since the doll museum was housed in a castle complete with stone walls, a drawbridge, stained glass windows and a moat it was not difficult to spend the rest of the afternoon wandering inside.

Except for a few dribbles, the storm was over by the time I was ready to go back to the campground for dinner. It had been a long, full and interesting day so I didn't mind spending another night in front of the television set.

On my way out of town the next morning I stopped to tour a prehistoric village. The site was an eleventh century, fortified pre-Mandan Indian village located on Lake Mitchell. An (indoor) guided and (outdoor) self-guided walking tour of the site lead to the first Archeodome Research Center that was built over a portion of the archaeological deposits at the village. I walked through a full-scale reproduction of an earthen lodge. Each section of the dig fascinated me.

I stayed the morning, lunched in their parking lot and headed to the largest grocery store I could find in town before getting back on the highway.

It didn't take me long to get a few supplies. I never purchased more than my little refrigerator and tiny cupboards could hold but I was fascinated to discover that South Dakota had a tax on food. That was the first time I have ever come across that.

I had a real urge to keep going west so I bypassed a few of the museums in Mitchell that didn't hold much interest for me. I drove less than a hundred miles when I came to Chamberlain and according to my AAA guidebook a 'must see' museum. I found my way to St. Joseph's Indian School and although we couldn't go inside to see the stained-glass windows depicting the Sacred Rites of the Sioux and the activities of the local Catholic church, the Akta Lokota Museum and Cultural Center was open. I wandered through the entire village stopping at each display. There were historical items and artwork done by the Sioux Nation. The AAA guide was right. It was definitely a 'must see.'

That night and the next I camped in Murdo and managed to spend a day and a half at the Pioneer Car Museum. Don't let the name fool you. The museum was made up of thirty-five buildings housing old cars, tractors and farm machinery. It has Elvis Presley's motorcycle along with the original registration certificate, coins, music boxes, guns, minerals and gems, buttons and bows along with memorabilia from the movie Dances With Wolves which was filmed in South Dakota.

Part of the museum was a street setting with old connected buildings made into a barbershop, a jail, a pharmacy and an office. As I wandered and spoke with other visitors the hours flew by.

I loved traveling through South Dakota. There was so much to see and do. The roads were in great shape. The people were friendly. There were more campers on the road and I was surprised to see so many with signs on them that said, "Alaska Bound" in big, bold, black letters. We all seemed to be heading in the same direction.

Chapter Twelve

Go Ahead and Make My Day

Seeing absolutely nothing from the road, I drove into the loop. I felt better after paying admission fees to the uniformed guard standing in the little house in the middle of the road. I knew that should I suddenly fall off the edge of the world someone would count the tickets and realize that eight thousand five hundred and forty-nine had entered that day and only eight thousand five hundred and forty-eight had exited. I was in the Badlands.

I needn't have worried. There were lots of people around and all were admiring the totally awesome sights. The area contains spectacular examples of weathering and erosion. Irregular ravines, fantastic ridges, low hills and cliffs displayed variegated color alternating with grayish-white sediment.

I also discovered to my sheer delight that they had a campground and before I went too much farther I booked into one of the sites for a couple of days. This was my first experience in this type of setting and where I fell in love with the National Park system.

At the Interpretive Center, suddenly feeling very outdoorsy, like camping from Florida to Alaska wasn't outdoorsy enough for me, I picked up a brochure and signed up for an outdoor, crawling-on-all fours, nose-in-the-dirt, lecture on tracking.

Donna, a young park ranger, had all sorts of goodies in her bag of tricks and we had to reach in and by feel alone guess what they were. She promised that there wouldn't be anything too unsavory but she lied. Things like a wispy snakeskin, a solidly packed robin's nest and a set of antlers were easy to recognize but an upchucked ball of fur and bones from an owl were another story entirely. On the trail we check out animal scat. Hunkering down close to our find I was suddenly thrilled that I had never had children. I just had to look. Didn't have to touch it, pick it up, wipe it up or change it. I looked, checked the chart and shouted out, rabbit's poop like everyone else.

Since the morning walk had taken hours, I skipped the afternoon walk in favor of a relaxing lunch but went to the evening slide presentation in the amphitheater. The subject was the buffalo and we learned that about five hundred roamed the park. That night I met Robin and Alex Sawatsky from Atlanta, Georgia. They listened to the presentation and enjoyed it as much as I did. Since they were camping in the same area I was they offered to walk me home. They had a flashlight. I didn't. I thanked them and accepted.

The next morning Robin knocked on my door and asked if I was going on the walk into the hills. I was just on my way out of the camper so we walked back, picked up Alex and were on our way.

Our ranger was Hallie Larsen and her specialty was geology but she was equally well-versed in regional flowers, grasses and fossils. Her outdoor lecture was terrific and the walk was a little more strenuous then the day before. I had my exercise for the day.

That night I shared a barbecued dinner with the Sawatskys. Their travels had been as extensive as my own.

ALASKA BOUND *and Gagged*

Robin worked part time in a travel agency just for the perks it provided. We shared our stories, horror and otherwise. Although we really just spent one day together they were exceptionally warm and caring people whom I would not forget and who would eventually play a very valuable role in my life as I would in theirs. In one disastrous rollover they would go from bit part players to lead rolls on life's dramatic stage.

I was out early the next morning. I watched as my friends folded up their tent, rolled up their sleeping bags and bundled up the trash and put it in the bin. We had coffee before parting. I waved to them as they took off in their black Ford Ranger. I packed up and left shortly thereafter.

To go from the spectacular of the Badlands to Wall Drug Store was a terrible letdown; however they did have everything I needed. It seemed they had everything that everybody else needed as well. According to the guidebook I had to stop. Wall Drug Store is a city block long with sit down restaurants, a grocery store, an ice cream parlor, souvenir shops, jewelry shops and neatly tucked away was the bank machine that I desperately needed. I put my card in and pulled out a bunch of money. I was solvent.

I walked the length and breadth of Wall Drug and on more than one occasion had a great chuckle, and before going too far, scooped up my daily dose of ice cream. As I ate I watched a mechanical singing cowboy quartet with a howling wolf in the background helping to serenade me. Everywhere I looked behind the plate glass something was moving. The cowboys were strumming their guitars. The wolf was baying at the moon. The stars were twinkling. An owl sitting on a branch in the tree was turning his head, hooting and blinking. I was mesmerized.

The story of the store's humble beginnings was posted on the wall. In 1936 the owners of the small-town pharmacy,

Ted and Dorothy Hustead, came up with an ingenious marketing campaign. Realizing travelers going through the hot, dusty prairie would be thirsty they put up signs along the highway offering free ice water. Tourists have been stopping ever since.

Within a couple of hours I was on my way towards Rapid City. Since it was still early in the day I decided to have my pictures developed at Wal-Mart in their one-hour photo shop. Unfortunately, unlike 'thirty-three or free' pizza joints, they do not guarantee the one-hour photo service. This particular one-hour service took two-and-a-half hours but the pictures were worth the wait. The camera was new and these were the first pictures that I had developed. The camera was definitely a keeper.

While waiting for my pictures I joined the throng of people at McDonald's for coffee. While sipping I looked around inside the crowded restaurant. An older gentleman caught my eye. He smiled when I looked at him and before I could look away he approached.

"Are you from San Diego?" he asked as he took the chair opposite me.

"No," I said. "I'm from the east. I just came from Toronto but I live part time in Florida."

"You look just like a lady I knew in California," he said.

"Well, if you want to go back about twenty-five years," I responded enjoying the company, "I did live in Los Angeles."

The conversation lasted a few more minutes before he took my hand, shook it gently and said; "perhaps I just like talking to a real pretty lady."

Just like Clint Eastwood in the Dirty Harry movies, he had certainly made my day.

Chapter Thirteen

Naked as the Day I was Born

The campground I chose was just on the outskirts of Rapid City since, according to my guidebook, there were no campgrounds inside Rapid City. It was located off highway 16 and the campground, although not mentioned as one of the attractions, happened to be directly right across the street from what was "Fort Hayes" in the movie Dances With Wolves.

I set up camp and walked across the street while it was still light. The store had been turned into part souvenir shop, part museum, and it made for interesting wandering since the walls were covered with pictures from the movie. I went back to my camper when hunger set in.

Before the night was over I had met almost everyone in the campground just by strolling around and saying "hello" to everyone who looked my way. The evening ended late, certainly by camping standards, and by ten-thirty I was dozing off, safely tucked away in my own bed.

It was the distant rumblings that caused me to stir. I think I fell back to sleep as the storm crept up ready to pounce. I awoke fully to a temperature that had suddenly dropped, leaving me shivering with the cold. I decided to pull the top of my camper down since the sides were made of canvas and did little to protect me from inclement weather. In order to do the deed I had to open the side door. When the thunder clapped overhead and a split second later lightning put on a spectacular show right outside my window I decided not to take the time to dress.

Naked as the day I was born I whipped open the side door, pulled the top down, dragged in the canvas sides hoping that nothing was caught up in the hinges and locked it into place. I put on a cozy tracksuit. I jumped back into bed and bundled myself into my blankets just as the rain pelted down in an icy stream. The storm did not sound nearly so fierce with the top down but the wind rocked my van from side to side and back to front. As quickly as the storm blew in, it blew out. I fell asleep to the music of gentle raindrops toe-dancing on the roof.

I brewed my coffee the next morning before opening the drapes. Fully fortified with caffeine I exited the van feeling a little sheepish. I was sure that everyone in the campground had watched me, totally naked, pulling the top down on the VW. I was stunned by what greeted me. Several large tree limbs had snapped. One beautiful hundred-year-old tree had been uprooted. Tables and chairs and picnic benches were scattered all over the campground. Two unfortunate campers did not retract the awnings on their motorhomes in time and had been ripped from the side, destroying the awnings and doing much damage to the side of the motorhome.

I could not believe that I had slept through the onslaught. I was delighted to realize that my little camper would probably hold back the devil himself if necessary. I hoped it wouldn't be necessary.

Chapter Fourteen

A Teaspoon to Dig a Grave

It would not have mattered how many days I spent exploring in the Black Hill area of South Dakota it would not have been enough. There was too much listed in the guidebook that I wanted to see.

My first stop was two miles south of Keystone to visit Mount Rushmore National Memorial with the sculpted heads of George Washington, Abraham Lincoln, Thomas Jefferson and Theodore Roosevelt. Created under the direction of Gutzon Borglum, he had intended they be sculpted down to the waist but died before the work could be completed. No further work was done at the time or after his death and no further figures will ever be added.

I stayed to listen to the story about Borglum by the Park Ranger and went through the mini museum that they had on site. Borglum was not paid for his work. Laborers were paid fifty-cents an hour (now you know why no further work was done after his death) and had to be supported in straps while holding and using a jackhammer. Their day started after they had climbed the mountain and were ready to go to work. Standing in the parking lot looking up at Borglum's creation was awe-inspiring. After seeing Mount Rushmore I knew that I wanted to tour Borglum's Historical Center. He had many other paintings and sculptures on display but needless to say nothing came close to the glory of Mount Rushmore.

The next stop I made was at Crazy Horse Mountain. Again, the site was so much more incredible when I heard the story and saw some of the scale models and exhibits at close range. I watched the movie being presented to get some scope of the work in progress and to learn a little about the sculptor Korczak Ziolkowski. The Crazy Horse Memorial was started at the request of Lakota Chiefs and represents North American Indians of all tribes.

Upon completion the figure of the Chief astride his pony will be five hundred and sixty-one feet high and six hundred and forty-one feet long, the largest statue in the world, much larger than all four heads on Mount Rushmore. The nine story high face of Crazy Horse was well underway but since I was viewing it from a mile away I was glad to have my binoculars.

The over ninety-degree heat of the day had been exhausting and I was glad to find my way back to my campground. I extracted my lounge chair from behind my window seat/footstool and planted it under a small shade tree. With novel and ice cold drink in hand, I plunked myself down on the chair and took the rest of the day off.

I just couldn't believe that I had to slow down my journey from Mitchell to the Black Hills because they had received a dumping of snow the week before. Thankfully that was all gone but it put me a few days behind schedule, whatever there was of it.

I could feel the morning heat and knew that it was going to be a scorcher like the last one. I studied my guidebook while enjoying my coffee and breakfast. I showered and was off to visit the Jewel Cave. I have seen too many caves to really be impressed with this one but the fact that it was forty-nine degrees Fahrenheit made the price of admission worth it. I stayed as long as I could and since everyone seemed to be doing the same thing I did not feel like I was loitering.....but I was. The afternoon held a once-in-a-lifetime treat. I drove one mile south of Hot Springs to the twenty-six thousand-year-old mammoth site believed to have been a sinkhole fed by springs. It is the only in-situ (left-as-found) site for mammoth bones in America. Mammoths, giant short-faced bears, and other animals entered the pond and became trapped in the mud. The slippery, steep banks made it impossible to escape. They died of starvation.

Some digging was going on and I hung over the railing to watch and could see the giant bones being uncovered. Guides were everywhere explaining the site's history and discoveries. I took hours wandering the museum. The tour and the lecture were very thorough. I went away wanting a teaspoon to dig with and a paintbrush to sweep away the dirt.

I drove the wildlife route through Custer State Park to get back to my camping spot. I stopped for a few minutes and watched antelope grazing in the fields. It was difficult not to want to pull over, turn off the ignition and spend the rest of the day watching the prairie dogs at play. They were so tame and seemed to be as fascinated with me as I was with them. Okay, I know they just wanted food but they'll sit up and beg just like a dog and stare at everyone and everything that moved. I loved it.

The buffalo in the park frequently caused traffic jams. I was waiting in a long line going nowhere and had no idea why. I finally turned off the motor. Fortunately I stayed in my vehicle. One huge male bison lumbered along the road in between the two rows of cars. By the time he was close enough to photograph I was scared out of my wits and fumbling with the camera. My hands were trembling like I had just had a Parkinson episode and I couldn't get my window rolled up fast enough. His giant head with a black, beady eye staring right at me and winking occasionally swayed back and forth as he passed my van.

This was one of the many times that I resented my solo adventure. The pictures of that giant wild beast would have been impressive with steady hands at the wheel and another pair of steady hands at the camera.

The last delight of the area was a day of driving the Needles scenic highway. It was a fourteen mile route threading through the oddly shaped, weathered granite spires from which the highway derived its name. There were several hairpin curves and one tunnel was so narrow I watched as a tour bus inched its way through. Even though I knew that he had done the drive a thousand times before I held my breath as he entered. There seemed to be less than an inch on either side as he drove through. He made it.....and I was sure he would.

Chapter Fifteen

If You Want to Eat You Have to Catch It

I needed a break from all the driving. I checked my campground book, was intrigued by the name of Fish N'Fry, went looking and found it. Driving the six miles (could have sworn it was at least double that) up and down the hills I realize that I should have read the ad a little closer and would have noticed that the campground was at a five thousand five hundred foot elevation. My VW was just about to run out of steam when I saw the sign that indicated that the campground was the next left turn. The driveway came up so quickly I almost flew (and I use that term loosely) past it. Thanks to some quick thinking, a lead foot on the breaks and a sharp left turn (thankfully no one came careening around dead man's curve towards me) I found myself picking up speed on the steep slope into their parking lot area. I could have laid out a yard or two of rubber as I stopped but I didn't. There was enough room to glide smoothly to a halt.

I found my checkbook and went into the office. The note on the desk said to find a spot that I liked, park and Randy would get back to me as soon as he returned.

I wandered around the store. They had a few necessities like milk, bread, cheese and lots of different candy bars. (Yes, to me candy bars, like ice cream, are a necessity.) They had the Deadwood daily newspaper for sale and a couple of old fishing magazines that anyone interested could borrow. They had a fully stocked kitchen, a couple of tables for your eating pleasure and loads of fishing poles in the corner. I was barely half way through the inventory when I heard a friendly "well, howdy. What can I do for ya?"

I turned quickly to say "hi" to the handsome, clean-shaven, dark-haired, late-thirtyish (possibly fortyish or fiftyish.....the older I get the younger they look) owner of the Fish N'Fry named Randy.

"Would you have a space for about four days for a small motorhome," I asked.

"How about right down there by the creek. Take your pick," he said. "If you're interested in a fish dinner, grab one of them poles in the corner. The pond is out back, well stocked with trout, and we'll fry it up for ya. It doesn't get any fresher than that," he said displaying a boyish grin.

Within minutes I was set up down by the creek, just at the end of the driveway, where I would have landed had I not made a quick right turn. I pulled out my deck chair to stake out my territory beside the only tree providing any amount of shade and went for a walk. I checked out the swimming pool. It was adequate with a large deck and padded lounge chairs for sunning. I walked from one end of the campground to the other, and waved or said "hello" to the few who were sitting outside. The four days, I decided, would pass quickly.

I spent the evening in front of a rip-roaring fire enjoying the company of two large families and their friends. I tasted, and instantly became addicted to, s'mores for the first time. This tasty treat consisted of graham crackers top and bottom, chocolate that melted the minute the toasted marshmallow was added to the middle. At fifty years old, who needed teeth anymore anyway? For my sweet tooth it was a perfect dessert. I will only admit to eating five or six of them but they were wonderful. Only my hips will tell the truth about how many I really ate.

The next few days was spent in total relaxation. I had stocked up on groceries so I never had to leave the campground. I labeled pictures. I wrote a couple of stories that, along with the pictures was eventually sent off to a Sarasota Newspaper called *West Coast Woman*. I swam in the pool every afternoon. I met almost everyone in the campground that was staying longer than a day or two, including a couple from the Boston area. When I told them my family name I discovered that Mark was a friend of my cousin who was born and bred in Boston. I gave them my business card and asked that I be remembered to my cousin even though I had not seen or spoken to him in about thirty-five years.

I played computer games and thanks to one of the ladies in the group I found 'spell check' on the computer and along with 'spell check' came the essential 'word count'. Up to that point I had been counting the words individually. It had been a relaxing but fruitful few days.....relaxing, that is, until the problems started with my van.

For no reason at all, or none that anyone could figure out, the alarm would go off. I was told that it probably happened due to the early morning dampness. I turned the alarm off manually. It went off again later that day when it wasn't damp. I turned it off again. I was in the swimming pool the third time it went off. One of the guys working in the campground disconnected it. That definitely solved the problem.

The next morning when I was getting ready to leave the van wouldn't start. Crawling under the camper Randy and his associate found a loose wire. They reconnected it, boosted the battery and off I went, almost like I knew what I was doing. I drove into Deadwood.

Chapter Sixteen

Boot Hill

I know I needed the few days of R and R but when I arrived in the town of Deadwood I chided myself for not having left the campground for a bit of touring. I parked my van on the only main street and slipped into what remained of the gold-rush boomtown. In the late eighteen hundreds Deadwood was a haven for gunfighters and gamblers like Wild Bill Hickok, Calamity Jane, Wyatt Earp and Doc Holliday. Hickok was shot and killed in Deadwood during a poker game.

I walked to Mount Moriah Cemetery (Boot Hill). It took a couple of hours of wandering around but I eventually found the grave of Wild Bill Hickok and lying next to him was Calamity Jane who requested that she be buried next to the man she loved. Hickok probably rolled over in his grave a few times over that one.

The hill getting up to the cemetary was so steep I thought I would have to be buried beside them by the time I arrived. Scattered around were other celebrities of that era like Potato Creek Johnny and Preacher Smith. With the help of a map, some markers and ample time to explore I found them all.

Before leaving Deadwood I took another hour or so and visited the Adams Museum. I could easily have spent the rest of the day there but I didn't allow myself that kind of time.

There were several floors of exhibits pertaining to pioneer life in the Black Hills. It was all displayed on the walls, on shelves and tables and glass case after glass case was crammed full of fascinating memorabilia from one of the most colorful times in American history. There was so much to see. I wandered until much of it became a blur.

I picked up a few postcards before leaving and, thanks to one of the postcards, have decided on a name for my van. The picture showed a rather mean-looking wolf with a caption that read, "you can't run with the big dogs if you pee like a puppy." My motorhome, a four-cylinder jobby with little to no poop for climbing hills no matter what their size, definitely "pees like a puppy." When I start referring to "the puppy" please remember that it is my van that I am referring to and not some two-legged or four-legged stray that I found along the side of the road.

I stopped at Roughlock Falls for a walk and some pictures and drove on to Spearfish where I stopped for gas and propane. I was told that the propane tank was the smallest that they had ever seen yet it never seemed to run out and rarely cost more than a dollar or two to fill.

I continued heading west. While the radio was blasting there was a sudden interruption to the music I was singing along with at the top of my lungs. "Severe weather was expected for south central North Dakota and the northwest corner of South Dakota." By the time I got through laughing and trying to figure out where they were talking about I was in Wyoming and close to Devil's Tower National Park.

Even from a distance it was an impressive sight. It is no wonder that they used it in the movie Close Encounters of the Third Kind with Richard Dreyfuss.

I pulled up to the office, decided to spend the twenty-five dollars for a yearly pass to all the National Parks, and went in to find a camping spot. I spent the evening enjoying the Park

Ranger's program, Devil's Tower in All Seasons, and when a sudden storm hit the area it was very frightening. We all scattered and ran for the safety of our homes on wheels. There was a lot of booming thunder that hit right above my rooftop. The lightning produced one of those spectacular shows that I just had to watch, with electricity that touched the ground. Eventually the wind, strong enough to rock me to sleep in my camper, blew past.

I spent the next day walking around the base of Devil's Tower and watched some climbers on the face of the Tower. It is a most impressive volcanic structure and all the sides are different.

I spent the afternoon cooling down in the van, organizing and labeling pictures and writing a few postcards. The rain started again around five in the afternoon and did not let up until it had totally ruined the evening program. I felt grateful that I had enjoyed the program the evening before and knew that it was going to be the same one. It didn't matter, I still felt cheated. I always managed to meet and talk with new people so I really wanted to be outside enjoying the show.

Before leaving the area I mailed my stories off to *West Coast Woman.*

Chapter Seventeen

Sixty-Five Endless Miles

The drive to Buffalo was a long and tedious one on a super highway all the way. Buffalo was a charming village with unique, privately owned stores, some looking very much like mini museums, and an outside wall on one of the stores painted with the backsides of horses tethered to a long hitching post. I fell in love with the place even before I had my walking tour. I ended up talking with an Air Force retiree, Paula, who had moved there in 1988 from the state of Washington.

"In 1988," she said, "Buffalo was a pee stop. Nothing more than a little black dot on the map with residents who were related to the original settlers. Since the 1987 drop in the stock market and the 1994 earthquake in Los Angeles, Buffalo has blossomed. I miss the old days," she said. "I'd love it if it stayed the way it was."

To me it still looked like a pee stop.

From Buffalo to Ten Sleep looked like an easy hop, skip and a jump and although I quickly ran out of gas stations on my way out of town I really didn't worry. It was only about sixty-five miles according to the map and I thought I had plenty of gas. It turned out to be sixty-five ENDLESS miles. What a nightmare!

I wished I had taken a closer look at the map. Perhaps I would have seen those green dots running along side a strand of kinky-looking red hair. Perhaps I also would have noticed that I was heading into the Big Horn Mountains and that I had to get over the Powder River Pass at a height of nine thousand six hundred and sixty-six feet. Perhaps I would have considered taking another route or at least looked for one. Perhaps I would have gone blindly into the mountains without giving life and limb another thought, which is basically what I did.

There was nothing I could do about it without turning back. I was barely half way there when The Puppy and I were not happy campers. I was scared again and I didn't like the feeling that my guts had twisted into a neat little bow being pulled tighter and tighter. The van would behave at the bottom of the gentle hills and lose power on the uphill splurges. At the top of each grade it would slow down to less than ten miles an hour. I was afraid to pull over to see the magnificent snow-covered mountains or to pick the tiny flowers that grew everywhere. I was afraid that it wouldn't start again and I would be stranded, freezing in the night air. There were very few cars on the road.

I was thrilled when the sign indicated that I was at the summit. The Puppy and I were both out of oxygen and eager for the downhill slalom run. My relief was short-lived. Just to keep me on the edge of sanity the van spluttered all the way down the other side of the mountain.

Had I known ahead of time that I was actually going to make it up and down without incident, I would have slowed down and enjoyed the fact that my van could only do ten miles an hour in high altitude. I would have stopped and smelled the flowers at a few of the rest areas, and when I rounded a bend, after driving what seemed like forever, and there was the snow-covered Big Horn Mountains right in front my me I would have enjoyed the view. It was incredible but I was just too scared.

When I finally got down the other side I wondered how my van was going to behave in the Rockies if it had trouble getting over this tiny mountain pass. I needn't have worried. The Powder River Pass in the Big Horn Mountains of Wyoming was the highest pass I had to cross and to this day remained that way.

I arrived in Ten Sleep, named by the Indians who traversed the Big Horn Basin of Wyoming and reckoned time and distance in "sleeps." It took ten sleeps to get half-way across the mountain. There was a line-up at the gas station and I was feeling extremely anxious. I kept going. I drove down the only main street in town. I passed a restaurant, a bar, a small all-you-can-steal mini-mart, and a campground and found myself out of town without even blinking. I didn't go far.

"What the hell am I thinking?" I said to myself out loud just in case it didn't register as a viable thought without being spoken clearly.

I turned around, checked into the campground, plugged in my services and went wandering around the town on foot. I found the ice cream parlor, my downfall, and with each taste slowly turned back into a human being. I walked back to the campground enjoying the last few licks of my double dose of pralines and cream cone and it was gone before I entered.

A Florida-plated truck and trailer had pulled in beside mine. Since they were just connecting their services I introduced myself to a minister and his wife from Port Charlotte, about thirty-five miles south of Sarasota, Florida. I told Tina and Tom about the ice cream parlor I found in town and they were eager for a walk after their long drive. We all trotted back. I tried to tell them that I had already had a double scoop but that didn't seem to mean anything to them. Without too much pressure I was convinced to have another. They had the pralines and cream and I had chocolate and peanut butter. We strolled slowly back to the campground noticing that there wasn't much else to see along the way. As we approached our campers, we said goodbye and each entered our respective homes.

It wasn't long before there was a knock on my door. "Nothing fancy," said Tina, "but would you like to join us for wieners in homemade chili and salad? We'll eat in about an hour."

I accepted and went into the office to see where I could buy a bottle of wine. The owner/manager, a giant, gorgeous dark-haired hunk, directed me to the bar in town since the town did not have a liquor store and the grocery store carried only limited provisions. I walked over to the bar, entered a dark little hovel and purchased a bottle of red to bring with me to dinner. It wasn't expensive and didn't taste half-bad.

The meal was a very pleasant-tasting filler and the wine and conversation flowed like we had been friends forever.

"Did you see that adorable sugar-pie in those tight-fitting jeans?" Tina asked.

"I sure did. If he's single my trip to Alaska ends right here." I said.

Needless to say the conversation between Tina and I continued on how we were going to find out if he was single or not. Tom chose not to be included in the matchmaking and let out a long, loud groan.

"Oh hush up Tom" Tina chided. "If this works out you can perform the ceremony."

When we were through eating, talking, joking and laughing we played several games of Rumoli. By the time I left it was after midnight, we were all exhausted and my anxiety was long gone.

We sat outside and had coffee together the next morning. When our hunk came by Tina asked, "Is there a supermarket in town?"

"No," replied the hunk. "You have to drive to Worland. They have a couple of them and it's only about twenty-five miles away."

"Is that where you and your wife shop?" she asked coyly.

"No," he replied, "we drive to Casper, pick up our groceries and visit our daughter at the same time."

"Oh, thank you," she said and looked my way giving me that "sorry, wish I had better news for you." She ended the conversation with the stud-muffin quickly and efficiently.

We were giggling even before he was out of sight, paying close attention to his backside as he walked away. We returned to their trailer, finished our coffee and said our good-byes.

We cleaned up, packed up and left. I went north west, delighted that I wouldn't be going far. They were heading east, back to Florida.

Chapter Eighteen

Seeing the World Backwards

The next day's drive was an easy one and I enjoyed every minute of it. I stopped in Worland to see a two-hundred-and-sixty-year-old Douglas fir tree that had been carved into a monument honoring the native Americans. I parked and got a close up view and took a few pictures.

As long as I was in the big city and there was a large grocery store within spitting distance I stopped and picked up some provisions to last a few days before driving on to Thermopolis.

I was stunned when I pulled into the State Park. The limestone travertine that holds mineral water, up to this point, I had seen only in Pamukkale, Turkey. Talk about seeing the world backwards!

I debated going into the free bathhouse. I really didn't feel like changing into a bathing suit for a mere fifteen or twenty minute soaking, which was all that they allowed. As much as I enjoy a liberating and relaxing mineral bath it didn't seem worth the effort. After watching for awhile, not seeing anyone go in or come out of the bathhouse, or any other attraction in the slide area worth staying for, I moved on.

I checked my camping guide for directions to the Fountain of Youth campground. I found the route, since there was only one main street in town, drove up the hill, pulled into the campground that had advertised a "huge mineral water pool." I checked in. I was shown where to park and drove down to my site. I was home.

The stay, as short as it was, was pure ecstasy. I spent the entire afternoon in the pool talking to everyone. No one seemed to be swimming lengths or laps and if they did want to swim it was just for a paddle or two. They were all standing with their backs against the wall in waist-deep water and talking.

I returned to my camper just long enough for one of my throw-together-and-hope-it's-edible dinners. It was such a beautiful evening. I cooked with the top popped up, all the windows open and side door yawning a giant hello to anyone that passed or looked my way.

When I went for a walk in the evening, I ran into a couple that sent me off for my still-damp bathing suit with the words, "don't leave all those wonderful minerals for everyone else. Get back into the pool," even though I explained that I had absorbed enough minerals that afternoon to open my own mining company. But how could I refuse! There I was back in the pool for another couple of hours. Fortunately they closed the pool at nine, otherwise I might still be there. Even after all those hours of standing and soaking, my skin wrinkled up like a shar pei puppy, it felt heavenly.

When I got back to my camper, just before dark, I discovered that another VW van had pulled in beside mine. If I felt like a hermit crab that had outgrown my shell I cannot imagine how my neighbors felt in their multigenerational condo on wheels. There were five of them, packed in like sardines and needing a shoehorn to extricate themselves, for an extra long weekend outing.

Their sleeping arrangements were explained to me when I looked at the crowd in utter horror. Mother and father took the lower bunk while daughter and son-in-law took the upper bunk. Eight or nine year old grandson slept in a hammock slung over the driver's seat. Needless to say no one went into the camper until they were knocked-out exhausted. We talked and munched, sitting around a roaring campfire, until well after midnight.

"What happens if it rains?" I asked innocently.

"We go home," Grandma answered without a hint of a smile.

My neighbors were surprised to see me in the morning. After spending about seven hours in the mineral water they assumed I would sleep the day away. Being of hearty stock I was back in the pool the next morning. I should have stayed on in the campground a few more days just for sheer pleasure of it but I didn't. After a leisurely morning soak I dried off, cleaned up, pulled the top down and took off. I knew that I wasn't going very far but the terrain left a lot to be desired.

It was a rather lonely road that took me to Cody, Wyoming with just one stop along the way in Meeteetse. I stopped at the gas station and ran into a couple that I had met in the pool in Thermopolis. Together we visited the Bank Archives and the Hall Museum. Before getting back on the road we had lunch and made plans to camp together in Cody.

I arrived in Cody early in the afternoon and checked into a campground right across the street from the rodeo grounds. Since signs were everywhere advertising that an Indian Powwow was taking place for the next three days, I felt it best that I check in early, since the campgrounds would be filling up quickly. There were two spots left in the one that was recommended. I took one and asked if they could hold the other one for my friends. The look on his face indicated that he wasn't thrilled with my request however, my friends showed up within five minutes of my arrival and I was still filling out the paperwork.

We set up camp, hopped into their car and just as we were leaving the campground we noticed that they were lined up on the driveway and out onto the street. We had arrived in the nick of time.

We drove down to the grounds where the powwow was being held. It certainly wasn't hard to find. The cars were lined up nose to ass on both sides of the street and we had a fair walk to park. It would have been just as easy to leave the car at the campground and walk all the way but it was too late for that.

We paid our entrance fee, walked onto the grounds and watched the dancing. The costumes were colorful.....all beads and feathers with matching tomahawks.....and the dancing, which was being judged, was powerful. The dancing wasn't even interrupted when some guy showed up on the grounds riding a buffalo.

That seemed to be a major difference between South Dakota and Wyoming. In South Dakota the buffalo roamed free. In Wyoming people were riding them. Later on that day, on our way to dinner, that same guy was riding the beast down the main street and in and out of the shops and bars. I know that it was all part of the show but these guys were tough. In Wyoming when they talk about 'a bull in a china shop,' they mean it. I wanted more.

Chapter Nineteen

Love Affair with Wyoming

Yippee-eye-oh-kaya. Love that rodeo!

The following evening Jim, Irene and myself dodged a couple of oncoming cars, sashayed across the busy street, do-si-doed a couple of hundred yards west, slapped down the six bucks which was the price of admission and swaggered onto the rodeo grounds.

We bypassed the popcorn machine despite the enticing aroma, the chocolate bars and the soft drink dispenser. It must have been early in the season or too many things going on in town but the stands were mostly empty. We took our seats about half way up so we had a great view of the entire goings on.

The spotlights came on almost immediately, like they were waiting for us. A steer was let loose and a cowboy was after him with a rope before we knew what was happening. Within seconds the animal was hog tied, released and another rider was on his way out of the shoot.

We watched the bronco riding, the bull riding with arms and legs flying in all directions and saw them race around barrels trying to make the best time. We marveled at the roping and when a rider was down the clowns came out to entertain and get the bucking bronco or snorting bull away from the downed rider. It was all so exciting, but the best, and I do mean the absolute best, was when they let the kids, under twelve years old, loose with a terrified calf that had a red ribbon tied onto its tail. Needless to say the winner was the one that got that red ribbon off.

Some of those little ones were no more than four or five years old. The tykes were all dressed in their best cowboy outfits, boots and all, and most wore a ten-ounce hat that was bigger than they were. They all started off keen and ran until they could run no more. They slipped in the mud. They tripped over their boots. They stood in the center of the ring and cried until daddy came and got them. They were the hit of the show and they were all rewarded with a ribbon for their efforts. No one got even close to the little calf. Everyone had a great time especially those of us in the audience.

Later that evening I learned that rodeo riding is taught in the schools and they all started young.

As if the daily rodeo wasn't enough for a small town, one of the most interesting museums I have ever been to was located in downtown Cody. Since the town is named for Buffalo Bill the museum sports his name as well and I had no problem spending a couple of days roaming from room to room.

The museum is broken down into four sections. The first section that I entered displayed the belongings of Buffalo Bill the showman, the scout and the pony express rider along with some of Annie Oakley's prized possessions. Exhibits provided insight into the American cowboy, conservation and dude ranching, and artifacts from the early west.

I took my time going through that section because, although I walked through the section called Cody Firearms Museum, I found little of interest. Since I purchased a two days ticket I left the rest of the museum for the next day. I returned early afternoon the next day and thoroughly enjoyed the Plains Indian Museum with an extensive collection of art, artifacts, ceremonial items and beadwork. The collection included dress and weaponry of the Arapaho, Blackfeet, Cheyenne, Crow, Shoshone and Sioux tribes. The exhibits depicted everyday life of these Plains tribes.

I ended the second day with a slow tour through the Whitney Gallery of Western Art studying paintings, sculptures and prints depicting the west. Artists represented were the best in their field, Frederic Remington, George Catlin and Charles M. Moran.

When I couldn't walk anymore I went back to my camper, back to the campground and enjoyed a barbecued dinner with some of the other campers. Jim and Irene had left that morning. I loved Wyoming and wanted just a little more time.

My love affair with Wyoming goes way back. I had been a tall, lanky fifteen-year-old when my sister got married in Los Angeles. When the wedding was over I refused to fly back to Montreal with my parents. I took a bus. When the bus stopped in Rock Springs for breakfast I preferred going for a walk around the town. When I returned from my walk I discovered that the bus had left without me. I called the next stop on the bus route and asked that they take my luggage off the bus and I would get there as soon as I could. I hitchhiked to Cheyenne. They rerouted my ticket and I was on my way. My first real-life adventure stayed with me all these years. I loved the memories. I loved the excitement. I loved Wyoming.

The following morning I was on my way again.

Chapter Twenty

One Touch from Disaster

It was warm and sunny and the drive into Yellowstone National Park would have been superb had it not been for the fact that my mind was preoccupied with the third anniversary of the death of my husband. Much of the scenery on the two-lane road into the east entrance was obliterated by the tears that filled my eyes before cascading like tiny waterfalls onto my cheeks and into an awaiting tissue.

My mind cleared when I paid my entrance fee and went looking for a camping spot for a couple of nights. I stopped into the store to ask about camping and was told that all sites were full but to drive down. "Campers leave all the time," she said. "You'll find something."

On the road south through the park all I saw were big red signs indicating that the campground was full. I kept driving confident that I would find something and slowly but surely became a little uncomfortable with my current situation.

I stopped for lunch by a stone wall with a little stream running under it. With yogurt and an apple in hand I left the van and walked over to the stone bench by the wall. Within seconds I was attacked so viciously by mosquitoes that by the time I scrambled back to the van, opened and closed the door behind me, my legs were covered with blood. I slapped, squashed and squished everything that moved for the next few minutes. I washed my hands and wet a paper towel to sop up the blood. I rubbed every visible inch with an alcohol-soaked cotton ball before putting some ointment on the welts to keep them from itching me to insanity (like that would have been a long trip!). I ate my lunch quickly in the van before continuing my trek south.

Eventually I drove out of Yellowstone, never finding an available campsite, and drove into the Grand Teton National Park. It was still early in the afternoon and I had no trouble finding a small, level spot for my VW in Colter Bay. I paid, slapped my receipt onto the pole and doubly protected my spot by putting my deck chair in the middle. I was delighted to discover that all the mosquitoes had been left behind in Yellowstone. None dared cross the border into the exclusive mountain resort of Grand Teton National Park.

With the promise of a continuing gorgeous afternoon I drove to Jackson Hole, a playground for the rich and famous. And that it was! It was a fabulous oasis surrounded by magnificent ski hills. I caught the odd glimpse of huge homes tucked into the hillside with, I must assume, beautiful people living in them. I had to assume because the only ones out on the streets, going in and out of every shop, were tourists. I parked on one of the side streets and joined the throngs.

The four archways into the city park were comprised of antlers that had been shed by the deer. The park had benches for sitting, flowers for admiring and walkways for strolling. I checked it all out.

Designer shops, art galleries, open-air cafés, souvenir shops and real estate offices lined both sides of the streets. People, cars and horse-drawn carriages were everywhere. My mini sightseeing tour was topped off with a giant ice cream sundae while relaxing in the park doing a little people-watching. I wanted to be back before dark. I left around four.

To add to the splendor of the day I stopped to watch a moose grazing in the fields on the way back to Colter Bay. I had no trouble finding my way home. I had a quick and easy dinner and went off to enjoy the evening program. There would be two this particular evening. The first one was about the porcupine and the second told the audience about Indian Heritage. Fortunately we all enjoyed the slide presentation and undoubtedly both would have been far more interesting with better speakers, however, when in my lifetime would I ever get that close to porcupine quills that were still on the pelt.

It was long after dark that I returned to my van, flipped on my television set to squint at a couple of fuzzy channels. While there was lots to do and see during daytime, the nights had my mind whirling. I did not sleep well and was plagued with nightmares.

I awoke early the next morning, relaxed over coffee and breakfast and cleaned myself and the van up in preparation of my day of touring. I put my chair out to again save my spot and headed north to Yellowstone.

Despite the fire in 1988 that damaged so much of the park, there was still a lot of wonder to behold. I drove all the roads around the park without stopping. I was just trying to get an overview. Up to that point the day had gone well.

I still had about twenty-five miles to drive back to my camping spot when the rain started, slowly at first. It was just spitting in fact. The intermittent windshield wipers took care of the problem but only momentarily. The sky turned dark and ominous. The heavens opened like there was a crack in the world. I suddenly found myself driving under an horrendous black cloud and no matter how fast my windshield wipers worked they couldn't keep up with the deluge. I could hardly see where I was going.

ALASKA BOUND *and Gagged*

My right wiper suddenly started causing problems, like a lazy eye that couldn't open all the way. It still worked but not in sync with the other one. One touch and the driver's side wiper was knocked out of kilter. What the hell was happening! This was not the time or the place! I wanted to scream.

The rain increased. The roads became treacherous. Mini rivers carrying mud and leaves washed down the center of the street reducing the traction as the van slipped sideways. I pulled off to the side of the road and into a mud flat.

My heart was pounding so hard it made my ears hurt. The throbbing at my temples threatened to bring on a migraine and I could feel the tightening in my jaw. Everything hurt.

I was suddenly desperate. I had to get back to my campsite. It was dark and getting on towards night. If I stayed where I was I would be alone all night, in the middle of nowhere and it frightened me just to think about it. I had to keep moving.

I inched my way, never getting out of first gear. I put my wipers on only when I really couldn't see and even then just one swipe then I turned them off. The passenger side wiper finally died. The driver's side was used only every few minutes.

"Please let me get through this nightmare," I prayed.

Chapter Twenty-one

A Good Deed

As if by magic the minute I left Yellowstone and entered the Grand Teton National Park the sun came out. Glorious, bright and warm and I could see steam rising from the pavement. My heart was still pounding as I drove but my breathing slowed ever so slightly. I knew I would make it. I suddenly felt like the hand of God was resting on my shoulder letting me know that I was safe. I kept moving, picking up speed as I went from second to third gear. I found the campground and my camping site and as soon as I turned off the motor my heart stopped pounding.

Before doing anything else I pulled out my manual and checked for a VW dealership within spitting distance or preferably closer. There was one in Jackson, Wyoming, forty miles south and if it wasn't raining the next morning that was where I was going.

I awoke early, had a quick bite to eat and headed for Jackson. I maneuvered some of the side streets and found the address I was looking for. The VW dealer had become a Geo dealer and I went inside to find out where they had relocated. I could feel the tears welling up and one of the young executives, who overheard me talking to the receptionist, asked what my problem was.

"I had a Volkswagen once. Perhaps I can help," he volunteered.

When I explained my problem, he said, "Easy as pie. Be back in a minute," as he disappeared through the 'employees only' door.

He returned with a screwdriver and a small wrench and guaranteed that he could fix the problem. "The wipers are designed to loosen before they damage the motor," he explained.

Within seconds the passenger side wiper worked as it was designed to. In my moment of grateful relief I forgot to mention that the driver's side could also use a little tightening and shortly after leaving the Geo dealer I tested the wipers. The passenger side was back to its peppy old self while the driver's side was indeed a little lethargic.

"Never mind," I mumbled under my breath, "I'll fix it at my next gas fill up."

I took the long way back to Colter Bay stopping long enough to enjoy the scenery and a ham sandwich and an apple for lunch. The spectacular landscape, caused by glaciers and earthquakes, had produced the Teton Range. As I watched, black clouds started to engulf the mountain. While I stood in cool sunshine a raging blizzard covered the highest peaks on the mountain. When the drizzle started leaving little splatters on my glasses I moved on.

I was safely back at the campground when a family of five moved into the site behind mine. Within minutes, mother and son belched away on a small motorbike leaving a wispy smoke trail, disappearing down the road and around the bend. They returned via another route. Ten minutes later two young guys whizzed by and disappeared. When they returned father and one of the boys was off and running. The motorbike mambo went on for over an hour.

At the first opportunity I approached the father. "You know," I said, "I have never known anyone who owned a motorbike that didn't own a complete set of ratchet tools."

With a big toothy grin Dan Strevey introduced himself and asked what I needed.

While he tightened my windshield wiper we talked about the park and the camping site. He caught me totally off guard with a direct question when he asked if I was traveling alone. I just nodded.

"Come join us for dinner," he said.

I thanked him for his invitation and at six o'clock when I saw his wife outside cooking and setting the table, I approached. "Are you aware that your husband is inviting strange women for dinner?" I asked.

"Yes," she said, "and we are expecting you."

I joined the family already seated at the picnic table bringing with me a huge pressure cooker filled with homemade soup and the remains of a bottle of white wine. Before Jacque resumed KP duties she introduced me to sons Scott, Jack and Daniel.

We gathered around the table and started dinner with my soup offering and fresh, crusty bread that I had picked up at the supermarket in Jackson. We had spaghetti, salad and apple pie for dessert. When my wine bottle lay like a dead soldier Dan opened one of theirs.

We told travel stories and shared our experiences in the wild. Just before dark, the ghost stories started. As night fell we moved closer and huddled around the crackling bonfire. When we had consumed more food and drink then was reasonable or necessary at any one meal I was reacquainted with S'mores.....the toasted marshmallow flanked by pieces of mint chocolate and sandwiched between two graham crackers. The mint chocolate added an entirely new sensation to my blossoming taste buds. It was sweet enough to keep any dentist in business the entire length of his career but absolutely worth every filling, every root canal and every false tooth that would be going into my head the minute the trip was over.

This simple act of kindness was one of my most treasured memories on this journey. Thanks to this caring and welcoming family my trip was back on track. I could continue my travels knowing that there were people like the Streveys out there.

My time in Yellowstone was coming to a close. I wanted just one more day.

Chapter Twenty-two

Old Faithful

My last day in Yellowstone National Park was a prizewinner. Before leaving the campground I visited the Colter Bay museum in the visitors center, walking distance from my site. The two floors filled with exhibits were examples of American Indian art and culture with emphasis on the Plains tribes. I watched the slide presentation.

I drove back into Yellowstone late morning to find Old Faithful. I was seated less than ten minutes when I saw the first sign of activity. With camera ready I snapped the instant I saw the spout hoping to catch several pictures at their various stages. It fizzled.

I watched intently and snapped a couple more shots at the next sign of life. It fizzled again. Each time it threatened to blow I aimed and fired.

Well, you guessed it. By the time Old Faithful was more than a three-year-old boy peeing in the wind I had taken my thirty-six pictures and didn't have time to reload before the spout erupted and hit the clouds. It looked like it was sticking its giant tongue out at me. I enjoyed the show immensely anyway and then bought a post card of the event.

I drove back to Grant Village to the see the movie about 'The Fire of 1988' and then drove on to the mud volcanoes. I had reloaded my camera by that time and took lots of pictures. Much to my disappointment they turned out flat and uninteresting even though you could see the occasional wisp of steam rising. There was no way to reproduce the smells and sounds and colors of the boiling mud.

As I headed north I stopped at the Tower Falls known as the Grand Canyon of Yellowstone. Again pictures could not do it justice. The Tower Falls where the presentation of the gorge, the falls of Tower Creek and the ridge of rock high above Yellowstone River have few equals. Only the real Grand Canyon would be more spectacular.

Just before the leaving the park I stopped at Mammoth Springs to walk amongst the travertine filled with mineral water. On a well-marked trail with some hand railing I followed the terrace-like formations created by the limestone deposits. My mind transported me back once again to Pamukkale, Turkey.

That night I camped in Montana.

Chapter Twenty-three

Up and Died

The campground, right on the main road, was not too far outside one of the western gates of Yellowstone National Park. The fact that it was so close to the national treasure upped the price by heaps and bunches. The land was flat. There was little grass, no picnic tables or swimming pool and no shade trees of any size. Nothing that I could see made a twenty-dollar per night price tag worth it except that they had, according to the brochure, an award winning bathroom and shower. Considering what we, as human beings, use a bathroom for perhaps no price was too great. Anyway I paid the twenty since I had traveled enough for one day, found my spot, and settled in nicely.

I called my sister from the campground pay phone. It was twenty-five cents for three minutes and I had a pocket full of quarters all lined up. I couldn't believe how fast the money was gobbled up. Since we got into a minor dispute I hated leaving the phone without a resolution. Mona wanted me to drive five hundred miles out my way to meet up with her in Salt Lake City, Utah. I tried to explain that I really wanted to be in Calgary in time for the Stampede. By the time my quarters were all gobbled up she was upset. I was upset. Before hanging up I promised that we would meet up someplace. I didn't know if she had heard my last words before being cut off.

ALASKA BOUND *and Gagged*

I walked the downtown area of Livingston the next morning. I picked up a walking tour map at the Chamber of Commerce. It was such a lovely old community with many historic buildings but I had such a terrible headache that I really couldn't appreciate it. The lack of sleep, with the conversation haunting me all night, had done me in.

By the time I got to Bozeman my head was pounding. I found a campground, checked in and paid, went out and did a little grocery shopping so I wouldn't have to leave the camp again that day or the next should it become necessary. I returned to the campground, closed the drapes, took a couple of painkillers, made the bed and fell asleep with the television set droning in the background. I must have been exhausted because I slept for several hours. I awoke groggy but without the headache.

I put my "hand knit sweaters for sale" sign in the side windows of the front seats and went for a long walk around the relatively small campground. There weren't many people to talk to so I just walked at a slow, steady pace, gradually clearing my mind.

When I returned to my camper several ladies approached including the owner of the campground. I was sure I would be reprimanded for the sign in my window but I was wrong. They introduced themselves and all wanted to see the sweaters. I laid them out on the picnic table for all to see. In the end I sold a couple and traded one of the sweaters for two nights in the campground. The owner was thrilled but not nearly as thrilled as I was.

Another that came looking was my eighty-one year old neighbor camping in a motorhome that seemed to dwarf my little van. She just looked and admired but purchased nothing. Later that afternoon I was invited in for tea.

Joei Carlton Hossack

She was from Connecticut and had driven solo to Bozeman. She had spent one week camping in Yellowstone and another week at an Elderhostel in the University of Bozeman, both of which she loved. She and her husband had purchased the motorhome a couple of years before and then "he up and died" she said.

"I had a choice," she explained, looking at me intently. "I could use the van, sell it, or let it rot in my back yard. I always felt that I belonged in Montana and I really wanted to see it, so when I had this opportunity I took it. I am loving the adventure," she confided.

The following day was devoted to the Museum of the Rockies. I couldn't believe that I had wandered so many hours that the entire day had just evaporated. It was one of the best museums I had ever seen. It was definitely on par or better than the Buffalo Bill Cody Museum in Wyoming. I started at the Bear exhibition, onto the Indian and then to the dinosaur exhibition. I wandered outside to an 1880 village before heading back indoors to the Indian paintings and a 3-D movie about the Badlands before finally ending it all at the Dinosaur Chronicles in the Planetarium.

It was an entertaining but exhausting day. I got back to the campground around seven, made a quick and easy dinner and relaxed in front of the television set for the rest of the evening.

I knocked on my neighbor's door the next morning as soon as I saw movement inside. The ticket into the museum was a two-day entrance ticket and I would not be using the second day. I offered it to her. She had not been there yet and was delighted. Since I will probably be arrested after someone in authority reads this section of the book I have decided to adopt a pen name. You can refer to me from now on as Miss Penny Passitalong.

ALASKA BOUND *and Gagged*

When Ruth, my next door neighbor, left for the museum I went for a bicycle ride. It was only three or four miles but I huffed and puffed all the way up the hill to discover that there was nothing but straight country road ahead of me. There were no houses or buildings as far as I could see. I finally turned around. Needless to say the trip down was a lot shorter as I went careening out of control. What little braking power I had finally slowed me on a small stretch of flat land.

I had been keeping the bicycle outside in the elements and it was being ruined. It was starting to rust. "Ain't gonna be worth much when this trip is over," I said out loud as I gave it an eyeball inspection.

As soon as I arrived the owner came back over to my camper. She had decided on another couple of sweaters and since my stay in Bozeman was almost over it was a cash deal. To keep in a productive mode I started writing the story about Wyoming. When the rain and lightening started I put everything away and relaxed over my television set. The rain continued all night.

Before leaving the area the next day I stopped at the Pioneer Museum to see memorabilia on favorite son Gary Cooper. Bozeman is where he went to school and since the museum was a former jail it was a fascinating tour. Many areas in Montana claim Gary Cooper as their own and little museums from different stages of life were all over the place.

When I left I drove through the back end of Bozeman. I had had no idea how large the city was and assumed that what I saw was what there was. I was wrong. I loved the business end of town with all the shops and restaurants and mini malls. I must go back.

Chapter Twenty-four

Uncle Sam

The drive to Helena was uneventful and when I accidentally ended up on the street with the Capitol Building I decided to wait for the guided tour that took place every hour on the hour. Historical paintings and statues decorated the interior and we stopped to look and get an explanation at each and every one of them. The tour still took only about a half-hour.

From the Capitol Building I found a Wal-Mart and waited while they developed a couple of rolls of film. I spent that night in a rather unkempt-looking campground right in Helena proper and that evening labeled all the pictures that I picked up that afternoon. I was delighted that I could do it while all the places were still fresh in my mind.

The next day I toured the downtown area on the Last Chance Gulch train. Since the date was July 4th Uncle Sam was with us on the train most of the way. We dropped him off at a private party on our way downtown. From the train we rode past the Government buildings, Reeder's Alley and finally made our way to where all the mansions were located. A local boy, who started a bakery business, put his name in the cornerstone of his building with the initials S.W.N. For those of us interested enough to ask we discovered that the initials stood for Started With Nothing. From such humble beginnings and lots of hard work the baker ended up with two mansions in the prestigious Gulch area. An hour after touring the Montana State Historical Museum I was back on the road again.

Except for a stop at a craft store in Augusta the drive to Choteau was thankfully, uneventful. Choteau, on the other hand, offered something rarely found in American campgrounds. I felt like I was back in Europe because camping was located in the center of town. I parked my camper and went out walking since the place was crawling (some literally, some figuratively) with other campers and picnickers. I also discovered the reason for the crowd and the merriment. A rodeo, within walking distance, was in full swing. I went into the stands to watch.

Since I arrived late I only saw what I thought was the last forty-five minutes. I whooped and hollered with the best of them and wished that I had brought my binoculars with me. I watched some of the roping and the bull riding until what I thought was the last ride. That last bull broke his leg coming out of the stall. The poor creature ran around the ring bogged down in mud, the back leg slipping out from under him at a horribly odd angle, and bawling. Even as I write, so many years later, I feel the knot in my stomach. Sick to my stomach and with many others I left the stands.

A single shot pierced the hoopla and all went quiet before I got back into my van. The rain started as I closed the door behind me and to get my mind off the events I started busying myself with dinner even though I felt more nauseous than hungry.

The rain amounted to nothing more than a few minutes of spitting and more campers arrived, one couple that I had spoken to in Yellowstone. Dinner was eaten at a large, shared picnic table and I brought out a bottle of wine. That too helped to get my mind off the rodeo events.

Joei Carlton Hossack

The group decided to go back to the rodeo and I didn't want to be sitting alone for the rest of the evening so I went. That's when I discovered that the rodeo went on as long as there were cowboys willing to participate. We all enjoyed it until the last event of the night. A young rider was bucked off a horse and broke his leg in the fall. He lay on the ground screeching for help. It seemed like forever before the clowns went in and caught the bucking horse and the paramedics could get to him with a stretcher. The ground was completely mucked up. We all watched in horror, rooted to our seats, listening to the screaming and knowing that there wasn't a damn thing we could do about it. We waited for the single shot that never arrived. He was finally whisked away in an ambulance that waited just beyond the back gate.

The entire group went back to the campground for a little more drinking. At around ten we returned to the rodeo stands for the fireworks display. After everything I had done that day, it was still the 4th of July and the fireworks lit up the sky for hours. I was neither the first nor the last to leave the next morning.

The museum in Choteau was a small one and I went through it quickly. Had I been willing to wait until two in the afternoon I might have been taken to Egg Mountain where a dinosaur dig was in progress. I was told that the work continued most, but not every, day. Since it was just a little after nine in the morning and they wouldn't know for sure until early afternoon if they were working that day I chose to continue my journey.

I drove to Glacier National Park stopping only once for lunch and to call my friend, Hugh Osler, in Calgary. It was terrific hearing his voice. He had heard from a number of our mutual friends who all wondered "where the hell I was." Without going into too many details I said I would be in

Calgary in a few days and we could talk all about my trip then. He was holding several packages of mail for me.

I drove the Going to the Sun road from east to west. Charles Kuralt was right. It was one of the most beautiful roads I had ever seen with waterfalls close enough to touch and snow-covered peaks far enough away not to worry about them. Goats and sheep grazed on higher ground. I camped that night in Apgar and it must have been at a lower altitude because I had no problem going for a bicycle ride. That afternoon I spent an hour talking to Milton Shiner, a gentleman from Seattle who collects first edition books. He made note of my name and promised to come to a book signing if I was ever in his area.

The evening program was very entertaining. The talk was entitled "Then and Now Glacier Park" but the ranger had a few jokes and anecdotes, not in the script I'm sure, to tell and made the talk far more interesting than it should have been. For the first time in quite a while there wasn't a hint of rain.

The next day I drove from Apgar to St. Mary's. The entire trip was only seventy-nine kilometers but it took over four hours, stopping to enjoy the scenery at Lake MacDonald and Logan Pass. I checked out many of the glaciers and stopped to watch the mountain goats that were grazing just off the path by the side of the road.

I hiked and biked after paying for my camping at St. Mary's. A ranger from Waterton Park, on the Canadian side of Glacier, gave the evening program. After a fine presentation he said he hoped we would stop and camp there. It brought back some vivid memories. My husband, Paul, and I had been there in 1990 after pulling a tent trailer across the country. On that visit it rained like I had never seen it rain before and we had to leave days before we wanted to because the inside of our trailer and more importantly our mattress had been soaked through.

I enjoyed the presentation. I also knew that I wouldn't be stopping on my way to Calgary.

This was my last night in the United States for awhile and I'd like to think that God was unhappy with my leaving so She cried. It poured almost to the point of flooding. The thunder was booming loud and right over my head. The lightening was a display of witch-like fingers with eerie glowing nails that struck the ground in so many spots it was hard to see them all. The wind, battering from all sides, rocked and rolled my van. I really thought I was going to be blown over but I could see that the tents across the way were still standing. It gave me some assurance.

By morning the sun was out.

Chapter Twenty-five

Calgary Stampede

I was rather excited about going to Calgary. Even though I didn't know Hugh Osler very well, he had been a great friend to Paul and I was anxious to sit and talk to someone who needed no background information. I looked forward to reading my mail. The idea of a soft, comfortable bed and a private bathroom complete with tub sounded right-down-to-the-bone luxurious and at this point in my travels I needed all of the above, which Hugh offered. I just need to get there.

I crossed into Canada just north of Glacier Park and since it was on the first day of the Calgary Stampede there was no line up and traffic, just before and after the border, was almost non-existent. The border guard was a very tall, muscular, handsome American Indian and for the first time an official was far more interested in if I had guns, mace, pepper spray, liquor and cigarettes than why I was traveling alone.

I stopped briefly in Fort McLeod for a walk about the compound and to take some pictures. I enjoyed a short version of the Musical Ride with the Royal Canadian Mounted Police in full-dress uniforms on their magnificent horses as they went out onto the streets of Fort McLeod.

I didn't want to disturb Hugh at work even though he said I should call when I arrived. I found a Wal-Mart to have my latest batch of pictures developed. I relaxed over a late lunch and picked up *The Milepost* after browsing for an hour or more at the bookstore in the shopping center where I had lunch. *The Milepost*, I was told, was the only book necessary for people foolish enough to attempt the Alaska Highway by motorhome and after thumbing through it I could see why. Every road in Alaska with every dumpster, every gasoline station, every campground, every dip in the road and every pothole had a separate entry at every mile along the way. I purchased it.

Once back in my camper I got out my Calgary map. I found Hugh's home without much effort and was out in front reading when he returned from work.

My few days in Calgary were sheer luxury. I was treated not only to a comfortable bed with a real mattress and box spring but my private bathroom had a Jacuzzi tub in it. Does life get any better than that? Well, yes it did. At a barbecue that night I met some of Hugh's neighbors, his girlfriend Tracye and Tracye's family. Hugh splurged for some scrumptious meals eaten in and/or taken out and/or dined out.

Hugh and I had some quiet moments. It had been three years since the death of my husband and I enjoyed talking about Paul to someone who knew a different side of him, a business side or an annual "cottage closing" side. It was a cottage closing that required eight guys, thirty-five minutes worth of labor and three days worth of drinking, fishing and card playing. Hugh and I did a lot of talking, laughing (a bit of crying) and some much needed reminiscing.

That evening we watched and bet on the chuck wagon races. An accident occurred during one race. One horse was killed and several riders hurt. I stopped watching. I didn't want to see any more events. Cody, Wyoming, Choteau, Montana and now the Calgary Stampede accidents had turned me off completely.

ALASKA BOUND *and Gagged*

When Hugh went to work the next day I went to the Stampede by bus. Every bus went in that direction. I spent the day wandering the grounds, in and out of every booth, eating hot dogs, warm cashews and cotton candy, a hangover from my schoolgirl days. I sat in the stands and watched hypnotist, Terry Stokes, work his magic with the audience. I enjoyed the dog show including all the mutts that performed. I took advantage of a free telephone call to a girlfriend in Montreal and had pictures taken with a couple of tall, handsome Mounties at my side.

The four days flew by and I knew it was time to leave the cocoon. I called Hugh to say that I was on my way out the door and he asked me to wait. He would come home and have coffee with me before my departure. We had a long talk. He made a couple of cappuccinos and by the time I left it was early afternoon. I stopped for groceries and a gas fill up and it was mid-afternoon by the time I was out of Calgary-proper. Even though it was a short distance into Banff I didn't want to risk not finding a campsite or wandering around in the dark.

I stopped for the night in Canmore, about eleven kilometers before Banff and was delighted with my choice. I passed a number of small craft shops before getting to the campground. My spot had a view of the spectacular Three Sisters Mountains and I settled in rather quickly. I put my bicycle into service and discovered that the campground was huge, the town was charming and the people, both in and out of the campground were friendly. I stayed an extra day. A German lady, Gerda, was so intrigued with my solo camping that she presented me with one of her hand-painted glasses. I wrapped it carefully so it wouldn't break on the trip. It was lovely and a perfect size for my morning juice.

Chapter Twenty-six

The Accident

The morning I left Canmore started well but went downhill rapidly. It was an easy drive to the entrance of the National Park and I had my money ready for him. Although I had the latest edition of the AAA guide I discovered that it was wrong and by a fair bunch. The fees had gone from five dollars per day to eight dollars per day and from ten dollars for a four-day pass to sixteen dollars or a three-day pass. The yearly pass had doubled. What had been thirty dollars before this latest edition was now sixty dollars and that amount was not mentioned at all. Had the numbers been a little more accurate in my guidebook I don't think I would have felt quite so ripped off. I purchased a three-day pass and grumbled all the way to the first spectacular sight, which wasn't far.

Banff and Lake Louise, both of which I had seen before, were still as beautiful and as crowded as I had remembered. When I went looking for a camping spot, still early in the day, I discovered that the camper that was ahead of me in line took the last available spot. After driving in circles for what seemed like hours I ended up in the overflow parking. It was absolutely disgusting and still cost seven dollars a night. Needless to say I was not impressed and wrote a nasty note to the park management that I included with my fee. The only pleasantry of the day had been running into Ann and Harry whom I had met and camped with in Choteau, Montana. By the time early evening rolled around even the overflow camping had overflowed. I was exhausted and had no problem sleeping that night.

After coffee with Ann and Harry I headed north. I was back in virgin territory and on my way to Jasper. I stopped often to marvel at the mountains or to check out my reflection in a perfect-mirror lake. Once, when I saw a motorhome with Netherlands license plates on it pull into a scenic rest area, I followed. I stopped to talk to the two couples. My husband and I had loved Holland and these people were as friendly in America as they were in their own country. The morning slipped by.

I stopped for lunch in a parking lot near the Columbia Icefields where I could enjoy another spectacular view and watched, through binoculars, as people walked on the glaciers. They were standing beside a regular-looking bus, with enormous balloon tires, that was parked on the ice.

Sandwich and coffee cup in hand, I walked up to the ice for my own little stroll. This was my first touch of a glacier. It was dirty white with bits and pieces of foreign matter imbedded into it. The deep cracks were various shades of blue, from a delicate baby blue to a marine blue. It was fascinating but I wished that someone would come along with a vacuum cleaner and make it more presentable-looking to tourists. After all this was what they came for.

Since I was still a long way from Jasper I didn't linger long. I had gone less than a mile from the Icefields when I came upon every cyclist's nightmare. A cyclist was sprawled, face down, by the side of the road. The first car that stopped was on a cell phone calling 911 and I had assumed, incorrectly, that a moving vehicle had hit him. I pulled out my sleeping bag and went back hoping that the man was not too badly hurt even though he had not moved since I first saw him. I heard him moaning as I tried to cover him. He wasn't moving but he was talking and vehemently refused the use of the sleeping bag. With much effort he rolled over and tried to sit up but couldn't.

Gradually his biking friends showed up and convinced him to accept the covering. He insisted that he was not in shock, that he wasn't cold and that he wasn't hurt. Obviously he had not looked in a mirror.

He had hit a rock on the road and would wait for the ambulance. The longer he waited the more pain he felt. The couple with the cell phone called 911 again and discovered that an ambulance was on its way but had been dispatched from Jasper which was over sixty-miles away. It would take a while.

This was definitely not the place for an accident. He did wait patiently and without complaining. We all waited with him and watched as he bled from many open wounds on his arms, legs and most visibly, his face. With all his friends around I could have left, however, I needed my sleeping bag if I was to be warm that or any other night. When the ambulance left I took back my sleeping bag and once again headed north. I had lost two hours in my drive and still had sixty miles to go. I was now concerned about finding a camping space in Jasper.

Even I was a little shaken by the accident. I stopped at Sunwapta Lodge for an ice cream cone and a look at the falls. The Lodge was where all the cyclists would be staying for the night. I waited while two of the girls called the hospital for an update. He hadn't arrived yet.

As I climbed back into my van and started driving I tried to keep my mind from dwelling on the accident. I realized that a serious accident on this road would spell disaster. No one could get to me in time. I drove slower and slower.

Chapter Twenty-seven

Getting Close

That night I camped at Wapiti, three miles south of Jasper and there were plenty of campsites available. The camping spots were on the pavement, something I didn't expect in a secluded area, but there were lots of people around and the television reception was better than I had seen in a while.

Walking through the park was a treat unto itself. The woods were full of grazing elk that didn't even look up when I got close and a coyote stole across my path about ten yards ahead of me. Small groups were strolling around checking out the wildlife and stopping to watch when they found something worth watching. Kids were playing, some bicycling up and down the paths. Older adults were sitting in clusters talking, drinking and munching.

I spent the next day in Jasper. I made my first stop of the day at the hospital. It seems my downed friend had been correct. He had not been badly hurt and apparently nothing was broken. He had been "cleaned up" and released. I was sure he would feel the effects of the mishap for quite some time and was not out bicycle riding around Jasper.

I spent the rest of the morning and early afternoon wandering around the town. I found nothing that overly impressed me especially with all the T-shirt and souvenir shops that lined the main street. I stopped for lunch at an outdoor café and enjoyed the scenery. The mountains around and the drive to the mountain resort had definitely been the best part of Jasper.

Before leaving, I drove around until I found a grocery store of any size and was definitely not impressed with a motorcyclist who pulled into my parking space as I was backing up into it. He looked back at me, smirked and gave me 'the finger'. I ranted, raved and swore at him until a small crowd gathered and reluctantly he moved. Gone are the days when female, fifty-plus, gray hair and glasses brings out the paternal instincts in barbarians. It did feel good, however, to exercise my vocal cords. Despite the fact that I never did too much talking I was still in 'fine screaming voice'.

I picked up some groceries, drove around the parking lot to see if there was a motorcycle worth running over, and finally drove out and returned to the campground. I found a few pleasant people to talk to and told them of the days events. I was definitely unimpressed with Jasper.

When the sun went down I spent my time writing letters, a few postcards and playing computer games while the television droned on in the background.

It was a long, uninteresting drive from Jasper to McLeod Lake on Highway 16 where I camped that night. I stopped only twice. The first time was to view the highest point in the Canadian Rockies, Mt. Robson, and to enjoy a picnic lunch. The second and much longer stop was in Prince George for an oil change, a propane fill up and another trip to the grocery store.

I ended up stopping a little earlier than anticipated because I had gone through a time zone. My watch said five and by that time had had enough driving for the day. It was actually four o'clock.

ALASKA BOUND *and Gagged*

I ended up in a Provincial Park directly across the path from Bea and Jake Hudson from Michigan. They were in a giant RV, the kind I usually refer to as a "small city." They too were on their way to Alaska but were having second thoughts. So many of the people they had spoken to found the roads atrocious with construction and roads torn up on almost every route. I just listened. I hadn't as yet spoken to anyone who had actually been there. Almost everyone I spoke to had heard a rumor or two about the conditions but nothing concrete.

The next day I would be in Dawson Creek, British Columbia, milepost "0" on the Alaska Highway. Even I was beginning to think, "I'm a little nuts."

Chapter Twenty-eight

Chain Saw Heaven

The drive from Whistler Camp to Milepost "0" was a pleasant one with only one stop on route. It was the town of Chetwynd. The area is famous for chain saw carvings and a map was available of their locations at almost every store in town. You can't miss the place. A full-sized carving of Mama Bear, Papa Bear and Baby Bear make you welcome as you enter the town. Goldilocks was noticeably absent.

I wandered around all the back streets. I found and took pictures of about a dozen of them. I couldn't help but wonder if the guy who massacred all those people with his favorite tool knew that there were other far more creative uses for a chain saw. Should I run into him on my way to Alaska I will certain tell him about it.

Dawson Creek had the charm of most small towns that have something interesting to offer. Before getting on the one road to Alaska everyone, myself included, wanted to see and take a picture in front of the original milepost "0" marker. The campgrounds were cheap and plentiful and right across from the campground that I stayed in they served the best and the highest ice cream cone I had ever seen for fifty-cents. For that reason alone I could have stayed a month or two but then my clothes would not have fit me. Come to think of it neither would my Volkswagen!

I spent one day visiting the museum/country store and watching the movie that was made while they constructed the Alaska Highway. The road was built in 1940 to get soldiers, supplies and food to the north when World War II broke out in the Aleutian Islands, just off the coast of mainland Alaska. I checked out all the memorabilia of that era and found a few too many things that looked familiar from my own childhood.

I was about to embark on a real adventure in a day or two. There was no turning back now.

After checking on protective screening and wire mesh to protect my grill and headlights at the hardware store, the feed store, K-Mart and Zellers I decided to check out *The Milepost*, which I now referred to as My Bible. I was happy to discover that one of the local campgrounds custom-made protective grilling. Before I ran myself ragged trying to figure out how I would do it, I would check with them.

I decided on a play day. I wanted a day to read, wash my van, visit with the campground owners, bicycle around and meet some of my neighbors. Two of the monster motorhomes were pulling out that morning and since I had met both couples that morning they suggested, since I was traveling alone, that I should travel with them. Actually it was the men that suggested I tag along. The women just glared at me.....then at their husbands....then back at me. I thanked them all, then spewed out a list of things that I had to do before actually getting on the road.

"You can catch up to us," said one of the men. "We'll be stopping at every gas station I'm sure. We'll watch for you."

From the look of the size of their motorhomes I was sure he was right.

That afternoon I found the campground I was looking for. I also found the owner Terry Bates. He said he was busy and could I return at six that evening. I returned at six to discover he was still busy and "would I mind waiting ten minutes." I waited close to an hour for him to discover that he was out of padding and I would have to wait until morning.

I returned at nine the following morning and he again asked me to wait. My patience was running low. So was his. He then advised me that the service he provided was for the customers of his campground.

"Had you told me that yesterday" I said, "I would have made other arrangements. This is my third trip here at YOUR request and I would appreciate the job being done so I can get the hell out of your hair."

"Wait ten minutes," he said almost as annoyed as I was, "and I'll do it for free."

I waited over an hour and gradually cooled down. While he worked we chatted. He was really quite pleasant and as fascinated by my solo travels as I was watching him string the chicken wire over the lights and grill with protective foam rubber to keep it from scratching the paint. Over the wire he put mesh to keep out the bugs. Plastic ties of every size held everything in place. It was all professional and protective looking.

"How much do I owe you?" I asked.

"Nothing," he answered. "A deal's a deal."

I pulled out a twenty (half of what the job should have cost) and put it in his shirt pocket. He thanked me and wished me luck. I smiled back and left. Like it or not I was on my way.

Before heading up the highway I stopped at the Pioneer Village with its turn-of-the-century buildings that had been refurbished and were currently in use as a restaurant, a candy store and a woodcarving center. Only the schoolhouse remained locked and empty.

By one in the afternoon I was really on the road to Alaska.

Chapter Twenty-nine

Liard Hot Springs

I camped that night in Fort St. John, around fifty miles from Dawson Creek. I was escorted to a spot right next to a midnight blue Westphalia, also with Ontario plates. We looked like we were having our own mini rally and that afternoon, after they had finished washing their rig, I met Michael and Christine, teachers on sabbatical from Toronto.

We had dinner together at the picnic table that separated our rigs. Once dinner was over we continued drinking wine. We had lots and lots and just in case I didn't make myself clear the first two time "**lots**" of wine. I discovered that they were both writing instructors and while we relaxed over the dregs that remained in the last wine bottle I got to read them some of my short stories. They were suitably impressed with my creative outlet while we were all getting suitably drunk. I'm not sure, but at that point they might have been suitably impressed with my reading of the Volkswagen manual. They might also have been suitably impressed with the fact that my mouth still worked at all.

The evening was wonderful and I don't quite remember how or when it ended but the stars were high in the sky and looked like fuzzy little bright things. We had finished all the wine and all the munchies that we both had in reserve.

ALASKA BOUND *and Gagged*

I know that the next morning started with my not wanting to hear any noise whatsoever. It was also much too bright for my liking. I prepared a couple of strong cups of coffee, which I downed with a hard, lightly buttered bagel. I wasn't eager to face much more. It was somewhere around eleven o'clock that morning that I said my good byes to Michael and Christine and just before leaving the campground I ran into a few other campers that I had met in Dawson Creek. We talked very quietly for a few minutes.

We all seemed to be going the same way and at the same speed and I was a little relieved. Before leaving Fort St. John I did a little grocery shopping and filled my gas and propane tanks.

The drive was scenic but slow. The road was very narrow in spots and although I ran into just a bit of construction I was definitely not in the mood for much driving. I had had too little sleep and too much wine.

At Pink Mountain I stopped for a stretch and a walkabout in Mae's Kitchen and for the first time ran into the two couples that had left Dawson Creek the day before me. While they had a late lunch I joined them in a coffee. With their big rigs they were indeed stopping at every gas station for a refill. Before leaving they wished me well and hoped that we would meet up again someplace but they were sure I would be traveling faster than they were. I stopped early that night in Liard Hot Springs.

I checked into the campground mid afternoon, changed into my bathing suit and set off to find the hot springs for which the place was famous. I was told it was across the road and through the woods. It was a well-worn path that I followed. I felt that whatever the cost it would be worth it. The cost was nothing. Yup, I was right. It was definitely worth it.

This was sheer heaven. I immersed in the hot water right up to my neck. It was luxurious. I let the water engulf me. I soaked up the minerals for over an hour, much of the time with my eyes closed. I relaxed my mind and my body and knew that if I stayed much longer I would fall asleep. It took my last bit of strength to get up and get out of the water.

I walked back to my van, lay down for a short nap and slept like the dead. I awoke a couple of hour later refreshed and ravenously hungry.

My dinner was an easy affair. There was no room for a barbecue, which I would have enjoyed, but I kept my trusty pressure cooker handy. Since it was easier and cheaper I became vegetarian as much as possible and in forty-five minutes could prepare, eat, wash up and be on to something else. On the nights that I ate alone it wasn't much fun. I ate quickly and usually with a book in hand or watching television. That night, in Liard Hot Springs, dinner was a solo venture and since electricity was an extra ten dollars that I didn't feel like spending I read during dinner.

I walked over to the lodge, adjacent to the campground, to see what was happening. They had a movie going on their video. I stayed and watched The Big Easy on their big screen television set. There were few people around.

Some of the guests returned all excited. A moose, one man said, was out grazing near the hot springs. We all wandered back to have a look. It was close to eleven at night and still daylight. We walked silently. I never saw the moose.

That night I went to sleep in daylight and awoke at four-fifteen in daylight. There would be another time change when I arrived in Alaska so there would be almost twenty-two hours of daylight. That was something I could definitely live with. I hate the dark.

Chapter Thirty

My Confidence Shattered

For the first time in a long time it felt wonderful to be traveling without a timetable or agenda. I awoke early and was back in the hot springs for a leisurely morning soak. I was surprised and delighted to see all shapes and sizes in the water. There were some engrossed in conversation, some sitting with their head back and eyes closed and others that smiled at everyone who entered. It was there that I met Jean Moore, who made her home in the San Juan Islands when she wasn't traveling. She didn't enjoy traveling alone and was actively looking for a male traveling companion. Her eyes twinkled as she regaled me with stories about "the rejects, the interesting ones and the ones that got away." We exchanged addresses just in case I found myself in that part of Washington State or she found herself in Florida. Since I wasn't planning on a morning nap after my soak I decided to leave when Jean left and we wandered back to the campground together. I changed, had a fast sandwich and was on the road within the hour totally refreshed and anxious to see what the rest of the day held in store for me.

I sat back in my seat, perfectly content with the drive and listening to the music on the radio, when the smooth pavement changed to the dreaded gravel that I had heard so much about. I slowed down at the numerous construction sites.

I pulled as far over to the right as I could when a vehicle passed and was delighted when each one went around and I had been struck with just a few small pebbles that, I'm sure, just nicked the paint. The dust that loomed like a giant mushroom cloud obliterated any chance of my seeing anything in front of me for the next fifty feet. I slowed down even more.

It was on that road that I learned that it was not the cars that pass me that cause the problem. It is the cars, trucks and semis that were aiming at me that did the real damage.

It sounded like rifle shots. When the first two hit almost simultaneously I ducked trying to get out of the line of fire. I was so sure that someone was taking potshots at me. I panicked. The second two hit in instant later. I slowed to a crawl, my mouth suddenly going dry and my heart pounding so hard it threatened to jump out of my chest. My windshield was sprayed again with small pebbles, dirt and grit as another semi raced past before I realized what had happened. I expected the tiny nicks and chips to crack my entire windshield and fall into my lap. It didn't happen.

The short drive from Liard Hot Springs, British Columbia to Watson Lake, Yukon Territory had totally changed my driving. My confidence was gone, as shattered as I expected my windshield to become. I wanted to turn around and go home. I suddenly feared every truck that came towards me. I wondered if the monster semi was going too fast and would skid out of control. I wondered what more damage it would cause to my windshield or my grill or my lights. I kept my side window closed fearing a rock would hit my arm as it rested on the door or, worse yet, hit my head and knock me senseless. I worried about everything from that minute on.

I discovered, too late to do anything about it, that even the young people who held up the construction signs were at risk. Those same trucks drove the same way past construction crews who would be showered with pebbles that would sting and bruise and occasionally draw blood. It was just a few truck drivers that caused the problems but their recklessness ruined it for a lot of us. I was now part of the masses with windshield damage.

Chapter Thirty-one

Another Single

By the time I arrived in Watson Lake I had run the gamut of emotions. The walk around the Signpost Forest was just the distraction I needed. A homesick soldier, Carl K. Lindley of Danville, Illinois, started the forest during the construction of the Alaska Highway in 1942. Over the years tourists have continued to add signs to the posts and when I visited there were over twenty-five thousand of them with about three thousand being added every year.

I wandered for over an hour. I turned one corner and ran into Richard Felton whom I had last seen and said hello to in Liard Hot Springs. He was alone. It didn't take long to strike up a conversation and to find out that he was indeed traveling solo. We talked and wandered and checked out the signs even getting to some of the out-of-the-way, long-forgotten posts. I stopped to take a picture of a sign with just one word "Mona" right in the middle of it. I wanted to send a copy to my sister, Mona, in California. The signs were fascinating and from all over the world. Some were nameplates. Some were city limit signs. Some were city names with populations. Some were license plates. Whatever sign that could be imagined became a loud voice for all homesick soldiers, lonely widows like myself, footloose and fancy-free couples on vacation or young, energetic free spirits. They were all nailed to any post with any available space at Signpost Forest in Watson Lake. I added mine.

For the first time since the Badlands, I enjoyed having someone to share the experience with, to talk to and to laugh with.

Since it never got dark it was difficult to calculate the time. We checked into the campground one next block over from the Forest and by the time we decided to share our evening meal the stores were closing. I ran to the grocery store while Richard ran to the wine store. We had a mere fifteen minutes to get supplies so we raced around like we were chased by the devil.

Since Richard's van was set up for sleeping and not for cooking I went looking for a barbecued anything I could find. I returned with steak and veggies and Richard returned with a bottle under each arm. We had both been successful. Richard produced a small freestanding barbecue, a bag of charcoal and matches.

There was a real touch of sadness that I couldn't seem to shake. This was what my life was like traveling with my husband. He did the outside work while I prepared the salad and the vegetables inside my van. A glass of red wine helped me not dwell on the past. By the time dinner was on the picnic table more than half the first bottle of wine was gone. I was finally relaxed.....and a bit tipsy.

While I was indoors preparing the food, the campground filled to capacity and my camping buddies from Dawson Creek, that suggested I tag along with them, had pulled in a couple of sites down and parked. While Richard and I enjoyed our dinner Michael went by and with a wink gave me the 'thumbs up' signal. I called Michael over for an introduction.

Before our dinner was over the other three members of their little parade came over for a glass of wine and a chitchat.

The men seemed pleased that I had "bagged a live one" and I now appeared to be a little more acceptable to the wives who viewed me as a little less of a threat. We finished our dinner under four pairs of watchful eyes.

We dined in the sunlight until after ten. We cleaned up and went for a walk around the lake or should I say part way around the lake, before going for a beer at both hot spots in town. Despite the fact that I hadn't seen all of Watson Lake this was definitely one of the larger towns along the way. It had two hotels and by the time we left for the campground the bars in both of them were closed. The evening ended with the first hug I had had in many months and it felt strangely uncomfortable and wonderful at the same time.

I awoke early and had some coffee. I walked around the town. From the Tourist Information Center I picked up several maps and a Yukon passport, which was free for the asking. I wandered back to the campground. I took a long, leisurely, hot shower.

Richard was just climbing out of his van for the first time. Since he still needed a couple of hours getting started and I had become the slowest driver in the northern hemisphere we arranged to meet in Teslin, approximately eighty-five miles up the only road.

The ride was slow, even by my standards. The roads were in poor condition with lots of construction. The vastness was intoxicating. In spots the road stretched ahead endlessly. I poked along. When I found an open gravel area off to one side of the road to enjoy my lunch, and there were just two other motorhomes there, I pulled off. The door to one of the motorhomes opened, a hearty "hi" echoed across the parking lot and I saw a hand waving me over. They were my buddies. I was invited in to join them for lunch. This time there were introductions all around. My hosts were Colette and John, Mike and Joanne and, of course, they were all eager to hear about my gentleman friend, Richard.

The piled-high roast beef sandwich with homemade potato salad, coleslaw, chips and a soft drink were so tasty that I was barely able to stop at just one. The company was delightful, even though I had to take a fair amount of ribbing. After much hemming and hawing I told them what I could. Although Richard and I had gotten into fairly lengthy conversations most of it was not of the very personal nature. He was in his late fifties, never married, no children and from England originally. He now made his home in British Columbia. He hoped to see the Yukon and Alaska in about six weeks with no schedule and no agenda. That was the extent of my information and I blurted it out in a matter of minutes.

During lunch I was told about a free campground nine miles north of Teslin. Since that was where I would be meeting Richard I would check to see if he wanted to stay at Mukluk Annie's. I was already intrigued by the name.

In the town of five hundred people Richard had no trouble spotting my van. I had locked all the doors and opened the windows and had fallen sleep in a parking lot on the main road. I obviously needed the sleep. With only a brief explanation it was decided that Mukluk Annie's would be it for the night. We stopped for a few supplies in the only grocery store available.

For those of us who travel a lot every once in a while we come across a situation so foreign that we might as well be on a different planet than in a different part of our own country. Our stop at the grocery store in Teslin was just such a situation.

While standing in line to pay for our groceries Richard flipped through a local cookbook. He came across a recipe for "moose head."

"What do you eat in a moose head….. the brain," he asked and answered in the same breath.

The person…..and I'm sorry to say I couldn't recognize if it was a man or a woman standing directly in front of me, turned and glared at us for a second or two. "No you don't eat da brain. Da brain is for tanning da hide," the person said, letting us know that he found Richard's remark totally ridiculous. "You eat da ears, da nose, good meat in da cheeks. You can eat da tongue. You don't eat da brain." The only word missing at the end of the long sentence would have been "stupid."

We couldn't wait to get out of the grocery store before we started laughing. I decided right there on the spot that the next time I find something or someone with a brain, I intend to tan its hide.

After shopping and filling with gas we found our way to Mukluk Annie's. Actually it would have been hard to miss since it was a large campground, a huge log-cabin restaurant/store and jutted out slightly right on the main road. The camping was free. Our choices were a large, deep-fried fish dinner plus a cruise on their boat or an all-you-can-eat breakfast. Since we had already purchased hamburger meat with all the fixings for the barbecue, we opted for the breakfast. Richard took out a bottle of wine which we now kept on hand for just such emergencies and toasted our good decision. Before the first glass was finished Michael and Joanne came over, beer in hand. We set up the barbecue for dinner. We were becoming a cozy little group, all six of us.

Over a long, leisurely breakfast with several cups of coffee Richard and I decided we would meet at the Sourdough Campground on the outskirts of Whitehorse.

Chapter Thirty-two

We Meet Again

Richard arrived at the campground about half-hour after I was set up. We were both eager to checkout beautiful, downtown Whitehorse. We went for a stroll. We passed the Pizza Hut, which was right next to our campground and I couldn't just walk past Tim Horton donuts, famous for the best tasting coffee in the world, so we didn't. We went in for a cup. I introduced Richard to my favorite blend, not yet available in the States, and, of course, what's coffee without a donut or two.

It was a totally exhilarating experience walking around the Yukon's capital and largest city. We walked and we talked. We checked out the stores and the restaurants on the main street. The satellite dishes, which seemed to be pointing at the earth rather than the sky, intrigued us. I had to know why. I went into one of the stores and asked the shopkeeper. It was explained that since we were almost at the top of the world, the satellite was "out" rather than "up" and that's where the dishes were pointing.

We found a vacant park bench, many of which lined the main shopping avenue, and continued our conversation. It felt good just to sit and watch the world go by however, within minutes, two familiar faces were approaching. They looked at me. I stared back at them, unsmiling, wondering if they would actually recognize me. They walked past. I continued to follow them with a stare. Robin turned around. I couldn't stop myself. I stood up and gave her a big grin.

"I knew it was you," she said as she hugged me. Got a good-sized hug from Alex as well and for a few minutes we talked about our meeting in the Badlands of South Dakota. I introduced them both to Richard.

Rather than make conversation standing on the sidewalk we decided to find a restaurant where we could sit and discuss our journeys. Their story was not a pleasant one.....rather terrifying, in fact.

They had totaled their Ford Ranger truck five hundred miles from nowhere, three days before. They had driven the length of the Dempster Highway from just south of Dawson City to Inuvik. From Inuvik they had flown to Tuktoyaktuk and received their certificate for dipping their toes in the Arctic Ocean. From Tuk they flew back to Inuvik, picked up their vehicle and headed south. They had just disembarked from the ferry crossing the Arctic Red River when the truck started skidding out of control.

When calcium chloride, which is used to keep the dust down on the road, mixes with water, it reacts like black ice. At the first sign of trouble Alex took his foot off the gas pedal. He managed to steer the truck back into the center of the road on three occasions before the truck caught an edge and starting rolling over sideways and continued rolling for three complete turns. Had it not been for the roll bar in the roof of the truck and the fact that the front windshield buckled out instead of in, they surely would have been killed.

Fortunately they had just gotten off the ferry and there were lots of people around to help. Someone in the group radioed for the Royal Canadian Mounted Police who were dispatched from Fort MacPherson and arrived in record time. Although shaken up, bruised and very sore in spots Robin and

Alex were not seriously hurt. They were taken to Fort MacPherson.

From Fort MacPherson they arranged with a trucking company to get their belongings out of the Ford Ranger and deliver them to their truck headquarters in Whitehorse. Robin and Alex would pick up their stuff in Whitehorse. Since a minivan, carrying tourists came into Fort MacPherson twice a week they managed to book passage to Dawson City for the next day. The hotel in Dawson charged a hundred dollars per night and the minivan ride for the two of them was three hundred dollars. They arrived in Dawson the day before the music festival started and their room was available for only one night. They left the next day for Whitehorse. This was the third day after the accident and there I was sitting on the bench. I must have been a sight for sore eyes.

When we met, on the main street, they had just come out of the travel agency. They had booked passage on the ferry going to Seattle, Washington. Since the ferry was booked solid for the next Monday they would have to wait eleven days before leaving Whitehorse. They didn't seem to mind since they had no idea when their belongings would arrive on the truck. They did learn that their minivan was the last vehicle to leave Fort MacPherson. The rain had started and the Dempster Highway had been closed.

We renamed that gravel highway to something far more appropriate. We called it the Dumpster from that moment on. In talking to some of the locals we learned that approximately three hundred cars, trucks and motorhomes per year rollover on the Dumpster Highway. Bear in mind that the road is only open about five months of the year.

I invited them back to the campground. We would all have dinner together. This started our plan of action.

Chapter Thirty-three

Back to Normal

We stopped at a small market on the way back to the campground and picked up a few extras just to spread my slim pickings around a little farther. As soon as we arrived I put my friends to work. Robin and Alex pulled a picnic table closer to my van. We covered it with an old sheet and before anyone could get too comfortable I retrieved a few glasses, a bottle of wine and we toasted our good fortune in being together once more. I took a couple of sips and left Richard to entertain my friends while I got out a box of crackers and sliced up some cheese. After taking a couple of crackers and a small block of cheese for myself I handed the rest to Robin.

I browned some hamburger, onions, garlic, celery and a few herbs in my pressure cooker. I threw in a can each of tomatoes, tomato paste and kidney beans and left it to simmer while I prepared a salad with the few vegetables that I had around and handed plates and silverware out to Robin who wasted no time in setting the table. While dinner simmered away on the stove I went outside to join my friends.

"Now this is normal," Robin said. "This I can handle," and she leaned over and kissed the top of Alex's head. "This is the first bit of comfort we've had since the accident," she confided. She looked at me, smiled and I could see tears welling up in her eyes.

As we wined and dined and talked I could see the blankness, more severe earlier in the day, leaving their eyes. We all, or so I thought, enjoyed the camaraderie.

Dinner was on the table by nine. The food and wine were gone by ten and we did the dishes around eleven. It was still light. I offered to drive them back to their hotel but they said they could walk. I got a hug and a kiss from both. I invited them back for breakfast.

I should have sensed that something was wrong but I didn't. Richard nodded at me, said goodnight and went into his van. I put the dishes away, made my bed and went to sleep in the gloaming, exhausted from a long, eventful day. It was well after midnight.

Before coming by my friends stopped into the travel agency. They decided that they would take the boat from Skagway, Alaska to Prince Rupert, British Columbia. It would be considerably cheaper. The baggage salvaged from their totaled truck would be sent to a warehouse in Vancouver and they would be there to get their belongings through customs. The shipping line would not charge them for storage.

"The people in the travel agency were so kind," said Alex. "We are so grateful for everyone's help," he said taking my hand and patting it.

They still had a week to wait for their stuff and I decided to wait with them. Without giving it a second thought I decided I would drive them to Skagway before continuing on my circle tour of Alaska. In the meantime we would all enjoy the numerous festivals going on in Whitehorse. This was 1995, the centennial year of the Northwest Mounted Police whose name was changed to the Royal Canadian Mounted Police.

Joei Carlton Hossack

There is only one road going around the Yukon and Alaska. North would take us to Carmacks, Dawson City over the Top of the World Highway into Tok, Alaska and then Fairbanks and south to Anchorage. The southern route would take us to Carcross, Skagway, and taking the ferry to Haines and Haines Junction before heading north to Burwash Landing and Tok. Either way we would be seeing it all.

I told Richard that I would be heading south to drop Robin and Alex off in Skagway at the ferry. He immediately informed me that he would be going north. Neither he nor I knew when he would be leaving. With his decision made, he became rather unpleasant to be around. Absolutely nothing pleased him. Since he didn't seem to want to talk about it, I did my best to ignore it.

The entire city of Whitehorse was dressed in its finery. There were parades and craft shows and flea markets and every store was open for business, with tables set out on the street. There was music in the street and the highlight of any Canadian festival is the Musical Ride performed by the RCMP and their magnificent jet-black horses.

Suddenly the campground we were staying in filled to capacity in one day. A single's camping club from British Columbia had arrived. I met several of the ladies. I asked if I could have their schedule so that I could catch up with them after I dropped my friends off in Skagway.

"Do you have a CB radio?" the leader asked in a tone that indicated that I would not be welcome to join them.

"No, I don't," I answered feeling somewhat dejected.

"Oh well," she said, "we'll just put you in the middle of the group and take care of you that way."

I thanked her over and over again. The roads had so intimidated me that I was delighted to think that I might have some company for the rest of my Alaskan adventure.

Eventually with all our talking Alex, Robin and I came up with yet another solution. We would wait for the truck to bring the stuff to Whitehorse. The bulk of it would be sent to Vancouver but the actual camping gear would come along with us. The three of us would see Alaska together, sharing all the expenses.

Chapter Thirty-four

Whitehorse

Through our last few outings Richard had become surly. In private he asked why I felt I had to drive "those" people to Skagway. I didn't feel he deserved an answer other than "they are my friends and they need help."

The four of us had one last dinner together. Richard and I went to the Follies and then out drinking and dancing. We did not enjoy the evening. I couldn't help but feel what a stupid, selfish man he was. If he had not been so disagreeable we could have delivered the Sawatskys to the ferry and then convoyed with or without the single's group. We would have had a hell of a good time.....and then again we probably wouldn't have.

I awoke the next morning with a note on my windshield and the space next to me vacant. I felt nothing but a niggle of annoyance. I half expected to run into him (hopefully with my van) someplace along the road. Fortunately for him I didn't.

With the decision made that I would not be traveling alone I felt much better. We could now really kick back, enjoy our time in Whitehorse and wait for their belongings.

We toured the S.S. Klondike, an enormous stern-wheeler boat that sits beside the Yukon River near the Robert Campbell Bridge. From 1937 to the 1950's it carried cargo and passengers between Whitehorse and Dawson. It is now in permanent retirement and a national historic site.

We watched the parades and clapped along with everyone else. We went in and out of every shop on and off the main street. God knows where we would have put anything if we had bought it. The Mounted Police stopped and chatted with all visitors. There were beanbag games on the main street. Ice cream was served and candies given out. The Mounties, for offenses like holding hands, walking arm-in arm or parking your car on rooftops, gave out souvenir tickets. There was a no-smiling law that was being enforced and almost everyone got a citation for that one. They had dog-sled teams to view and horses to pet. And every day we went to the storage company to see if their goods had arrived.

We were all together the day the manager of the storage facility called. Their stuff had arrived. I waited in the van while Robin and Alex went in to check what was still useable and what was damaged beyond repair. They set things out to take with us while the balance would be shipped to Vancouver to wait in storage until they arrived.

They decided quickly what they absolutely needed and what they didn't. Since they would be driving with me and we would need at least a month to see Alaska they made arrangements to ferry to Vancouver on the twenty-eighth of August. I would return them to Skagway for the sea journey. Since no sleeping accommodations would be available at that time, they would need their sleeping bags for the ferry trip as well.

We loaded up my van to the point where I couldn't see out the back window. I transported them back to their hotel room. Their afternoon would be taken up with sorting and resorting what they would need for our trip and repackaging what would be sent on to Vancouver. When I picked them up for dinner that evening they were both totally depressed.

They had so much stuff with them they knew they couldn't fit it all into my van and still have some degree of comfort. They had bags with clothing. Some came with us, some went back into storage and some were thrown out. They had sleeping bags and tenting equipment, which was an absolute must, since they could not afford a hotel or bed and breakfast every night. They had boxes of food that we could use. The boxes and bags made up an endless line that stretched across the floor of their room. We just prayed it would fit.

We had dinner at the Pizza Hut. We walked around town. We ended up at a bar just off the main street because the music, stuff from the 60's and 70's wafted out to the sidewalk. There were a few people dancing and while we stood in the doorway, waiting for our eyes to adjust to the darkness, the band motioned for us to come in and grab seats up front. We were singing along even before we found our seats.

The waitress bought us some beer and when the band broke for intermission a couple of the guys came over and sat with us. They wanted to know where we were from and how we were enjoying the Yukon and if we had any favorite songs. The bar was nothing to brag about but what great fun we had! It was near closing time when we left. The Sawatskys walked me back to my van and then walked to the hotel.

The next morning I called my sister in Los Angeles and told her where she could find me on the map. She was suitably impressed. I told her that even I was impressed since most people just mortgage their home for a cruise to Alaska or they fly to Alaska, stay in hotels and take guided tours everywhere.

"I can't believe that I actually drove here," I gushed.

"What does the place look like?" she asked. "Is it cowboy? Is it primitive? What's it like?"

ALASKA BOUND *and Gagged*

"Mona," I said, "the campground is next to the Pizza Hut and the Pizza Hut is next to Tim Horton Donuts. This could be anywhere in Canada or the United States for that matter." I also explained about the satellite dishes pointing down rather than up and that it looked so strange.

When I wrote to her later that day I told her that I would be traveling with a group. I knew that it would ease her mind to think that I was not alone on the trip. I did not tell her that the group would be traveling IN my van.

We purchased our ferry tickets from Skagway to Haines. We attended some dedication ceremony and ended up meeting, enjoying and going out to dinner with Irv and Marge from Ontario. They were driving a brand new, less than a month old, Winnebago. I will never figure out why someone would buy a brand new van, especially after doing some research, and take it on the roads in Alaska. I'm sure by the time they returned to civilization and decent roads they would need new 'everything from the windshield down unless, of course, they ran into hail in which case they would need everything new from the windshield up as well.'

Later that same day two Hymermobiles from Germany pulled into the campground in Whitehorse. Man-oh-man were they a long way from home......then again.....so was I.

Chapter Thirty-five

Ménage-a-Trois

July twenty-sixth was our first day on the road as a ménage-a-trois. We had spent most of the morning packing the van. They really did have a hell of a lot of stuff but the only really uncomfortable one was Robin. She was sitting on the back bench-seat with everything piled up around her on the seat so she couldn't move. She had her seat belt on so she really couldn't move anyway. Every square inch of the floor was covered with something. Much to her credit she never complained. She read from the guidebooks constantly letting us know what we were seeing and telling us what would be around the next and every corner to come.

I, personally, was thrilled to have the company. They assured me that they were equally as thrilled just to be able to see Alaska in relative comfort and minimum expense. Alex really wanted to do the driving. I explained that I'm a lousy passenger and, much to his disappointment, would let him drive only when I was really tired. As much as I hated to admit it, and certain did not voice my confession out loud, I was a little leery of having him behind the wheel. After all, it had been just days before that he had totaled his own vehicle.

Our first stop on the drive to Skagway was Carcross. The town had a couple of hundred people and was interesting to stroll through the streets seeing nearly every front yard filled with rusted, used and broken cars, trucks, refrigerators or pieces thereof. A few of the residents tried planting gardens, but niceties were few and far between.

Carcross, formerly known as Caribou Crossing because of the large numbers of caribou that traversed the narrows, also had a visitor reception center and we discovered, almost too late, that this was one of the places to get our Yukon passport stamped. I had to dig mine out from some little cubbyhole since I never really believed that I would see much of Alaska by myself.

We dined at a picnic table outside the visitor's center and read the guidebook. Carcross is famous for having the smallest desert in the world. We went to take a look and stopped to check out Sandy Beach on Lake Bennett.

From Carcross south we headed back into British Columbia for a few miles and then crossed over the border into the United States. From the driver's seat I could see directly into the office at the border crossing and after declaring who, what, when, where and why, I asked if we could go into the office and see the articles that had been confiscated. They had leopard skins. They had a panther penis that was supposed to be ground up into a powder and sprinkled onto God-knows-what and was supposed to act as an aphrodisiac. They had a superb collection of ivory carvings.

The drive down the Chilkoot Pass into Skagway was a brake-burner. It was tough to keep my foot off the brake pedal but I could almost smell the rubber burning. I put the van in low gear and practically inched my way down. We stopped often to see the sights and spent quite a while at Dead Horse Pass to read the history.

The Chilkoot Pass was thirty-three miles of pure hell that the gold miners had to climb to get to the Yukon gold.

Since part of the journey was through Canada the Northwest Mounted Police parked themselves at the border and would not allow any miner to pass that did not have a thousand pounds worth of supplies. The thirty-three miles had to be climbed many times before they had the required amount of food and supplies. This was done because Dawson City in the Yukon, where the gold strikes were made, had ballooned from two hundred residents to three thousand squatters when the Gold Rush was at its peak. The area ran out of food and people were dying from starvation.

All of Skagway is a National Park. The town with a winter population of three hundred is infested with tourists from the day of the last snowfall to the first flakes of winter. The town is ringed with snow-covered mountains. The end of the main street is the dock landing and the harbor is never devoid of large cruise ships and ferries. We saw all the movies and slide presentations that the park service had available. We had several walking tours just to see if different guides showed different places. We took lots and lots of pictures. I took one picture of the back of a van that said "Lost in the Yukon." Poor fellow had no idea how lost he really was considering the fact that we were in Alaska.

Our camping spot was right across the road from the train station that took tourists from the cruise ship up the Chilkoot Pass. Robin and I stood there waving at the passengers and they all waved back at us like we were part of the attraction. We were laughing so hard we thought we would wet our pants.

One morning we took a four-mile walk out to the cemetery. I enjoyed a bicycle ride through some of the more outlying streets after lunch, watched another slide presentation and took another walk with a ranger later in the afternoon. Every walk centered on a different location. Every ranger concentrated on a different subject and each one had his or her own unique stories to tell. All of them were enjoyable.

Chapter Thirty-six

The Card Game

One doesn't have to dig too deeply into the legends of the north to find out about "bad guy" con man Soapy Smith, who died in a gunfight in July of 1898. Since Robin, Alex and I had seen his gravestone at the Gold Rush Cemetery on an early morning walk we were anxious to hear the "real" story. We spent the evening at the Eagle's Hall. It was there that the 1890's came alive with a snappy-looking Soapy-in-the-flesh along with raucous cancan dancers, Belle Davenport and toe-tapping ragtime music.

When we purchased our tickets at the door we were each given five hundred dollars in chips and escorted to the gaming tables for a little blackjack. We split up so we could each come away big winners. Betting was heavy. It didn't take long to get down to my last few dollars and towards the end when I had sixteen showing and asked the dealer, dressed in a gay nineties costume, for another card she peeked at it and asked "Are you sure you want another card?"

I declined. She added a king to her fourteen and she was over. I grabbed the chips, flush for the next few hands. When I asked if I could shuffle the cards she handed me the deck. Needless to say my money and everyone else's lasted until the show was ready to start. All the dealers were part of the show.

ALASKA BOUND *and Gagged*

We found our seats in the second row of the theater; every single one of them eventually occupied. Every seat in the small theater had a great view. Audience members became part of the act. The story was fascinating. The acting was as good as could be expected. The music was loud. The cancan girls were energetic and terrific. The evening was fantastic, a real winner. We stopped for a drink on the way back to our camper and relived each moment.

We were up early the next morning and on our way. It was a short ferry ride to Haines (thirteen miles from Skagway by water, three hundred and sixty-miles by road) and made even shorter by the National Park Ranger on board who filled us with information about the Inland Waterway.

We didn't stray too far from Haines. We took a city tour with a park ranger. We did some sightseeing on our own. We spent an afternoon at the museum. We shopped for a few groceries and another bottle of wine and had our first real dinner treat. Another camper had been fishing that day and had been overly successful. They supplied us with a large salmon, which they had cleaned but were unable to use. It was manna from heaven.

I cut off the head, peppered the cavity and shoved some chopped onion and lemon slices into it. I wrapped the whole fish in a couple of layers of tinfoil. In another couple of layers of tinfoil I put two large sliced potatoes with some chopped onion. I salted, peppered and olive oiled the package and both went onto the barbecue. I made a salad.

We're talking gastronomic ecstasy here! We ate and drank for hours, not wanting a morsel of that pink and flaky salmon to go to waste. We were also waiting for the sun to go down but it never did. It was around midnight that we cleaned up and went to bed.

Haines was a wonderful little town but a day or two was all we needed. We slept late. Breakfast consisted of bacon, eggs and toast on the barbecue. We did some grocery shopping and got back on the road.

It seemed like such a simple pleasure, and I know I keep repeating myself, but I enjoyed having someone to talk to, to share the spectacular scenery with, to prepare a meal with and for, and to help with the cleanup chores. It was also nice to have the occasional in-depth conversation.

All of Alaska waited for us.

Chapter Thirty-seven

The Hot Tub

The day was almost totally uneventful except for the incredible scenery with its snow-covered mountains and awe-inspiring vastness. There were few people on the road and by myself would have been extremely intimidating.

We stopped at what turned out to be a deserted campground. It was lunch time and since it was warm and sunny we decided on a leisurely outdoor picnic. Robin found a checkered red-and-white tablecloth at the bottom of one of her many bags and covered one of the old and splintered wooden tables. She set out the silverware and plates and I handed her some cheese, a variety of meat slices and a package of hoagie buns. We no sooner had everything set than motorhomes, vans and cars started coming in off the road. Our once deserted picnic area now had people crawling all over the place and not all were as classy, dignified or as sober as we were. When lunch was over we moved on.

We stopped at the Visitor's Center in Haines Junction, Yukon Territory for an award winning slide presentation on the glaciers in Kluane National Park.

Our campground that night was also an award winner in my book. How could I resist a campground called the Cottonwood that advertised a hot tub? We checked in, found our site and settled in. While my friends set up their tenting equipment, I had to hunt for my bathing suit which I found crumpled up at the bottom of my bench seat storage unit. It lay directly underneath my high heel shoes and pantyhose, both of which I doubted if I would ever be using again.

This was splendor amongst the trees. We were situated right on a lake. The majestic, white-capped mountains were all around. The hot tub sat on the patio calling to me like a seducing lover. I ran to it with open arms and a heavy towel around my shoulders to protect me from the late afternoon chill.

The air was cool. The water in the tub was hot and the steam immediately fogged up my glasses. I laid them on the side of the tub. The other guests in the tub were from Switzerland. I spent the most glorious hour.

My traveling companions ended up talking to people in the laundry room since that was their action for the night....laundry. We ended the evening with a cup of herbal tea and watching a most glorious sky.....striped pink and blue. I could have stayed a week but we didn't. After one night it was time to move on.

The drive, straight through to Tok, was breathtakingly beautiful with snow-covered mountains in the distance. There was not much traffic and not much construction. Because of the rain the roads were lousy with muck and mire but we made it.

The campground was terrific. We were not only treated to a movie about the area but a speaker as well. For the past fifty years this elegant little lady has made her home in Alaska. A week after getting married, someplace in the lower forty-eight, she was brought to Fairbanks and flown to the Arctic Circle to teach school. She was a very entertaining speaker who didn't let the rain deter her from her lecture but it was starting to get very cold. She didn't stay around long for the question-and-answer period. By the time she autographed a few of her books and left the platform the rain felt like stinging ice pellets.

The rain assaulted us all night. The Sawatskys had a miserable night and didn't sleep much. Their bedding got wet. It was all packed up in the rain. My van felt cold, damp and nasty and my little electric heater did little to alleviate the problem. We had a couple of cups of instant coffee and then breakfast in the van. It was still raining when we left Tok.

By the time we stopped for lunch the rain had abated. The Richardson Highway to Valdez was in great shape with only few potholes and no construction. We drove the Old Richardson for a while and stopped at the Tourist Information Center for a video.

It was hard to understand why Alaska wanted statehood. It is so unlike anything else in America. It was easy to see why it is called "The Last Frontier." It is wild and restless, peaceful and all consuming. Even people living in total isolation, of which there are many, need others around to survive, even if those others have four legs ending in paws.

The road to Valdez was spectacular. We stopped at Worthington Glacier for a stroll along the path and a walk on the glacier. We stopped for pictures. As a group this was our first of many glaciers. We stopped to take pictures at Bridal Veil Falls and Horsetail Falls before getting to our final destination for the night, home of the 1989 Exxon disaster, Valdez.

We camped at the Eagle's Rest and after dinner went for a walk around the town. Before retiring for the evening I tried calling my friend, Jackie Donoho, in Anchorage. Her answering machine was on. I didn't wait for the message to finish. I hung up and would try again the next night.

Chapter Thirty-eight

Alaska Pipeline

August arrived without ceremony. We spent the early morning relaxing, reading and having breakfast knowing that we were in for a treat. The tour bus picked us up right outside the campground office door promptly at ten-fifteen. We were headed for the marine terminal where the Alaska Pipeline tour started. Valdez is mile eight hundred and the end of the pipeline.

En route the driver regaled us with amusing stories about Alaskan statistics. Valdez has about ninety inches of rain and about three hundred inches of snow per year. The previous year almost doubled that amount. The government also did a survey about why people stay in Alaska. It seems that ninety-five percent of the people living in the region are alcoholics and the remaining five percent never sobered up long enough to finish the survey. Unfortunately a lot of truth is said in jest. Alaska is the number one state for alcoholism. If Alaska was a country it would be ranked fifth in alcoholism in the world. Although everyone laughed as the driver filled us in, they were very sad statistics for such a beautiful state. He finished his monologue just as we arrived at the terminal. His timing was perfect.

ALASKA BOUND *and Gagged*

While on board we had a complete tour of the outdoor facilities, however, only at the observation tower were we permitted off the bus. We had a non-stop informative commentary about each section of the pipeline. There were several ships in the harbor ready for refueling and we could watch the process from a distance. Fortunately I brought along my binoculars that I had to share with my friends, but we could see everything clearly and had enough time for viewing.

Since 1989, when the Exxon Valdez ran aground on Bligh Reef causing an eleven-million-gallon oil spill, the ships have protection around them to prevent oil from spilling over into the surrounding water.

Just outside the marine terminal gate was a bronze sculpture created by Californian Malcolm Alexander commemorating the efforts of the men and women who built the trans-Alaskan pipeline. Fortunately we all had our cameras and enough time to focus them properly, so we took home some crystal-clear mementos.

Mid-afternoon was spent at the Tourist Information Center watching a movie about the Good Friday earthquake of 1964 that registered nine point two on the Richter Scale. This was the first of many screenings and each showed the disaster from a different angle. Waves caused by massive underwater landslides swept over and engulfed the Valdez wharf taking thirty-three lives with it. Though much damage was sustained in the downtown and residential areas, only the waterfront was completely destroyed. Valdez was moved. The relocation was approved in 1964 and the last remaining residents moved to the new town in 1968.

The Alaska disaster produced tsunamis and other coastal disasters all the way down to the South Pole.

We were busy preparing dinner when a rather interesting-looking gentleman ambled over from his site. We invited him to join us for dinner and drinks. He regaled us with humorous stories for hours until Robin and Alex excused themselves to go for a walk. By the time they returned, which seemed like a life-sentence later, I had listened through five wars, three ex-wives, a pack of ungrateful children and umpteen jobs to go along with various homelands. I prayed that he still had his collection of war-memento service revolvers and would execute me on the spot instead of torturing me with more stories. I excused myself and let Robin and Alex listen to him for a bit longer while I went back into my van and closed my eyes instead of trying to sleep with them open.

Just before pulling out the next morning another camper handed us about five pounds of freshly caught, filleted salmon. We thanked him. Wrapped the fish in tinfoil and found a spot for it in the refrigerator. We knew that it would be another gastronomic delight dinner but that was a long way off. We were back on the road again.

We took the thirty-three mile detour to Chitina. There was a diner, closed until lunch, a bunch of old, rundown, never to be opened again, used furniture shops, what looked like a machine shop that would open if you needed him and a couple of streets with relatively well-kept houses on them and that was all. A sign pointed the way to McCarthy, sixty miles down what looked like an unforgiving stretch of road. We had seen a movie on McCarthy and although it would have been interesting taking a hand-cranked basket over the water into the town, the sixty-mile drive to the basket would have done us in. The road was gravel that had been put down over old railroad ties. We drove a mile or so down the road and decided that if I had a dozen or more spare tires (on rims) I might have attempted it but a mile with my van rocking and rolling all the way was enough. The other fifty-nine miles was out of the question.

ALASKA BOUND *and Gagged*

We stopped for the night approximately one hundred and fifty miles before Anchorage. We should have stopped earlier for groceries because there was nothing around. The campground was almost empty. There were no stores. There was one restaurant that was grossly overpriced and I had very little surplus food. I ended up using some of the fresh salmon with a tin of shrimp, a tin of clams, a can of tomatoes and lots of herbs and spices. The seafood goulash was heaped over noodles.

"If this is what you can do with almost nothing, the rest of your meals must be a feast," Alex commented.

I would have preferred the salmon cooked over the barbecue but there was no wood around and I was completely out of charcoal. Even I couldn't complain.....the meal was delicious.

During the evening I read some of the stories I had written. I'm not sure if they were impressed with my writing or impressed with the fact that I was the owner of the van and we were still one hundred and fifty miles from Anchorage. They listened intently. There is nothing I like better than a captive audience and they knew they were in for it when I said, "Come into my parlor said the spider to the fly."

We had no idea of the time. We were still going to sleep in daylight and, no matter what time we woke up, we woke up in daylight.

The next morning we left the campground in the rain. It drizzled all the way to Palmer.

Chapter Thirty-nine

Square Dancing Tonight

A sandwich board at the front gate said "Square Dancing Tonight" in big black letters and, after the long miserable drive, we were all keen for something new and different to do. As we checked into the campground the dark clouds that had plagued us all day turned darker and more ominous. There was booming in the distance. A lightening strike lit up the sky.

The day-long drizzle had turned to showers. Robin and Alex set up their camping equipment quickly before everything got soaked. There had been so much rain around and on so many consecutive days that my companions' spirits were as soggy as the ground they had to sleep on. They tried not to let it show and I couldn't blame them for being disheartened but it was the only way they were going to see Alaska. There was not enough room for the three of us to sleep in the VW Westphalia especially for people that were just traveling together and not really, really close friends or relatives.

While the Sawatskys set up their camping equipment I prepared dinner. By the time dinner was on the table, the inside of all the windows were fogged up and dripping with condensation adding to the clamminess. We ate quickly, did the dishes, got out our umbrellas since the heavens had literally opened and dumped, and walked to the long house at the far end of the campground where the dancers were just starting to gather. Just inside the door a greeter made us feel welcome and asked if we were square dancers.

"Did a bit a long time ago," I answered, "but I'm really here just to watch. I love the music."

Robin and Alex said that they were just going to watch and had never done any dancing, although they were willing to learn.

The dancers were very friendly. Everyone came over to say hello and a few even introduced themselves. When a gentleman approached and asked me to dance, I declined politely. He refused to take "no" for an answer. So I made an attempt.

It did not go well. They went left. I went right. They went right. I went left. During that dance I never got straightened around. I was thrilled when it was finally over and sheepishly went back to my seat and the safety and security of my friends who offered nothing in the way of encouragement.

The lady dancing directly across from me came over and "gushed" over my feeble attempt. "You were wonderful," she said all enthusiastically and seemed to want to chitchat.

I swear I thought she was being sarcastic. "They went left and I went right. They went right and I went left. What was so wonderful about that?" I asked.

"That's your partner's fault," she said. "He should have lead you better. Girlie," she said very seriously, "you're in Alaska now. Women don't take the blame for anything."

A smile, a hug and I was ready, willing and able for anything or anyone that came along. The next dance was for everybody including those who had never danced before. They gave us a quick lesson. The dance was slow and easy. We didn't sit down for the rest of the evening.

Alaska life was suddenly growing on me.

Joei Carlton Hossack

We drove to Anchorage and checked into a campground in the middle of the city. I called my friend Jackie. Since it was a local call I listened to the entire message on her answering machine hoping to get some idea as to when she could be reached or perhaps where she was. Jackie was a friend from Florida and she knew that I would be in Alaska sometime during that summer.

After the usual "can't come to the phone right now" the rest of the message was for me. It said, "Joei, welcome to Alaska and its shitty weather. Call my daughter Deborah for further instructions" and she gave the phone number.

I called Deborah and was told that Jackie was in Europe and that she, Deborah, had the key to her mother's house and I was to stay at her home. I mentioned that I had some friends with me and she said, "great, then you won't be lonely. Where are you? I'm on my way."

"We're in a campground in town. Come on by and we'll have dinner together," I said.

"I can't today, I have stuff to do. Why don't I pick you up tomorrow morning and we'll have breakfast together. Then I'll take you to Mom's house," she said.

Deborah came by bright and early the next morning. We followed her to Jackie's bungalow. We each picked out the bedroom we wanted and Deborah made a pot of coffee. We sat around the kitchen table like normal human beings and relaxed like we had been there forever. Deborah didn't stay long. She had some chores to do and left. I unloaded some of the groceries from the refrigerator in the van and Robin brought in some of her things and put them in her bedroom. While I was playing with the appliances trying to see how the stove, microwave and toaster worked the phone rang. It was Deborah. She invited us to dinner. She would pick us up around four in the afternoon. I accepted.

ALASKA BOUND *and Gagged*

Alex, Robin and I had a quick and easy breakfast with real toast and margarine that actually melted on it. Alex turned on the colored television set and while I lazed on the couch, Alex took the Laz-y- Boy recliner and Robin took the rocker. There was no question about the fact that we were making ourselves at home and spreading out into every room of the house.

I couldn't resist the bathtub any longer and soaked until my skin wrinkled up like one of the old Florida babes who sit in the sun from early morn until dark. Robin refilled the tub the minute I vacated the bathroom. We were in a house and it felt sooooooooooooo normal.

There was something so special about that evening and my Alaskan friends. They were a little more open and friendlier than most. They were a little more hospitable and a little less pretentious. The conversation and the wine flowed all evening. Deborah worked for the City of Anchorage and husband Ken was a self-employed computer programmer.

We were delivered back home well past our bedtime.

Chapter Forty

A Walk on the Wild Side

We spent three busy, fun-filled days in Anchorage. We toured the downtown area one day, checking out flowers planted everywhere, including on roof tops, that were at least double of size of any we had seen in the lower forty-eight. We spent part of the morning at the Tourist Information Center. We watched one movie on Denali National Park and another on the Earthquake of 1964.

Since it was National Airplane Day and Alex was a former pilot we spent a warm and sunny afternoon watching old airplanes taking off and landing, some on terra firma but most on the water. The three of us sat on a park bench, surrounded by the old planes, worshipping the sun God. We were in seventh heaven.

On a second day we went shopping. We went into every department store, every shop selling T-shirts and sweatshirts, every gift shop, every ice cream parlor. Had we purchased anything we would have needed a shoehorn to get it into my van. The weather had been so terrible for so long that we just enjoyed being outside and seeing the sights.

We stopped at one of the outdoor vendors for a quick bite to eat. I had a Rudolph the Red Nose Reindeer bratwurst. Okay, okay so it wasn't Rudolph! It was just a plain old reindeer bratwurst. It was still delicious, very lean and not terribly spicy.

That afternoon we traipsed through the Alaska Museum. The glass works of Dale Chihuly, taking up the entire first floor of the museum, were fabulous. We looked at every piece from every angle, most of them too heavy to lift without a crane. We went through each room studying the work for design and color, and in the last room hundreds of smaller pieces were displayed on top of glass that was suspended from the ceiling. To see it properly you had to lie on your back and roll from section to section. Would have been a good place to stop and take a nap but there were too many others waiting to roll over you.

The lobby of the museum had one last Chihuly masterpiece. It was a giant chandelier that hung from the ceiling to the floor with what looked like balloons filled with water. Not that it made me uncomfortable to look at it but I had the feeling the whole thing should have been wearing a giant, multi-level brassiere that needed to be hiked up some. Every woman standing there looking at it gave a little tug.

The second floor of the museum showed life in Alaska done in paintings and sculptures.

After the museum we went to a large cemetery to see giant whalebones that were used as tombstones. We walked the entire cemetery and read the inscriptions on many. They died young up there. Out in the wilderness, life is harsh. Anchorage is like any other big city but twenty miles out of the town and it's a different world.

On the way back to the house, not going even one street out of our way, we stopped at a Volkswagen Dealer to see what was available on the lot. There was nothing of interest.

Our last night in a house in Anchorage we vegged out in front of the television set. It was amazing how easy it was to slip back into old, bad habits. We were all perfectly content.

Before hitting the road for the south we learned that the National Ferry System was not going on strike as was previously reported. Alex called a travel agency and we all booked passage from Skagway, Alaska to Prince Rupert, British Columbia for August twenty-eighth. We were now on a schedule. We had twenty days to visit the rest of Alaska. We hit the road right after breakfast. We were barely out of Anchorage when the drizzle started.

Chapter Forty-one

Ice Worms.....Fishing Anyone?

We stopped at Portage Glacier. Even having to stand outside in a driving rain that threatened to change to ice pellets as it peppered our faces was worth the sight. The distant ice cap that dropped right to the water's edge was fabulous. The icebergs, with a tiny portion sticking above the water and the bulk of it under the surface, gave us a chilling account of what happened to the Titanic. When we were close to freezing and hopping around in one spot while patting ourselves didn't warm us enough to feel anything other than mini-glaciers clogging up our arteries, we went into the Visitor's Center. We started to steam when we walked into the overheated building. My glasses fogged up immediately.

In the theater we were shown a movie about the Harding Glacier. When we were finally comfortable and reasonably dry we wandered around the center picking up brochures and reading the wall plaques. Sitting on the reception desk was a large, glass bowl with a chunk of ice in it and a sign warning us not to touch. On the mini-iceberg wriggled a number of ice worms. One touch from a warm finger, we were told, would incinerate them. We watched in total fascination.

I held my index finger poised at the top of the bowl and threatened the ice-worms with annihilation if they didn't listen up. The neatly dressed guard sitting behind the desk was not amused.

The drive to Seward would have been far more enchanting if it had not been raining so hard. There is a thirty-five foot tide in this area so at low tide much of the landscape was mud flats. We saw none of it. We really couldn't tell if it was high tide, low tide or just flooding rain as we made our way to the outskirts of Seward. The campground we stayed in had hostel-style rooms available. Robin and Alex rented one of them. The rain continued through dinner in the van, colored television in the lounge and then most of the night.

The next morning we drove into town. We found the largest grocery store for some supplies and then walked into the Tourist Information Center and listened to some guy ranting and raving about the fact that there was supposed to be square dancing around and where was it. He had been following the square dance circuit and was really enjoying his trip, until this fly in the ointment. He too had been traveling alone. It certainly put some intriguing notions into my head.

The ranger at the Tourist Information Center of the Kenai Peninsula did a wonderful job of explaining volcanoes, plate shifting and earthquakes of the region. Back outside the rain continued to beat down on the van and our spirits. It was another soggy night.

We walked through town the next morning before getting back on the road. It was nine miles out of our way to Exit Glacier but well worth the drive. The rain stopped just as we arrived. We walked right up to the glacier, making note of how far this one had receded over the last hundred years. We stood or sat on the ice and took some unbelievable photos.

We had lunch at one of the picnic tables in full view of the gently rolling glacier that seemed like it should have been used for children sledding down the mountain. The scenery was simply so far removed from anything I had ever seen before. Spectacular is the only word that comes to mind to describe it.

We drove to Homer, mostly in sunshine. It didn't take much to change the mood in the van. The sun certainly did the trick. We rounded the bend in the road and directly across were the most beautiful snow-covered mountains. We had to stop because it literally took our breath away. This was the same view we had from our campground early that afternoon.

We parked the van. Robin and Alex set up their tent. We took out our deck chairs and in total silence just looked out at the awesome scenery. Late afternoon was spent walking the main street of town. My friends treated me to dinner at a Chinese and Sushi buffet. We left the restaurant stuffed to the gills.

The following day Alex went halibut fishing. Robin and I went to the Homer Spit. Homer is host to a large artist community and many were sitting outside on the decks working. Potters, sculptors, painters and jewelers practice their craft in full view while answering questions or talking to friends or tourists. They then sold their goods in the local shops and galleries.

We visited all the shops. We talked to all the shop owners and realized that there were really only two different shops. Both of these unique shops specialized in bone, scrimshaw and carvings. Only the native people are authorized to work with bone and tusks. It is illegal for all others.

It was late in the afternoon when we were making our way back to the campground. We stopped at the Tourist Information Center, picked up a brochure about the art galleries and discovered that one of them was right next door. They had some interesting basket weaving but not much else.

Alex returned around seven glowing from having caught five fish and having seen two humpback whales and some otters. As rough as the sea had been, and there had been some huge swells that Robin and I had seen from the shore, he had a wonderful time and really enjoyed every minute of the fishing expedition. The refrigerator was now totally stocked with the fish that we didn't eat for dinner that night.

The following day was for visiting all the art galleries that were listed in the brochures we picked up. We drove the gravel road to the top of the hill, overlooking the Spit, for some picture taking. Homer was not only an artist's paradise but a photographer's nirvana as well, assuming of course, that the weather cooperated. It did not. It was cold, windy and the drizzling had just started as we got out of the van. On the way down we stopped at Homer High School and saw the complete skeleton of a sperm whale suspended by wires from the ceiling that a local fisherman had found a couple of years earlier. After an early lunch I drove Robin and Alex down to the harbor. They went on a puffin boat ride.

The weather was much too cold and nasty for me to be on a boat. If you haven't already guessed, I am not much for being on the water unnecessarily, and especially not on a small boat, or in a big boat, or when it's cold, or when it's too sunny.

Meanwhile back at the ranch, excuse me, wrong book. Meanwhile back at the van I had no sooner set up my computer than Mike and Joanne (my Michigan friends from Dawson Creek) pulled in. We all walked up to the office for some coffee and parked right beside the office/store was another little blue Westphalia, just like mine, with Ontario plates (my friends Michael and Chris and one drunken evening in Fort St. John). What a hoot!!! That's where Robin and Alex found us, many hours later, when they returned from their puffin expedition. They thawed out their frozen fingers on a hot cup of coffee.

The rain kept us from enjoying a halibut barbecue so we all went out for Chinese food again.

ALASKA BOUND *and Gagged*

The drive back to Anchorage was rather uneventful except that we stopped once again at Portage Glacier. We were stunned by the difference that four days had made. The little bit of sunshine that we all enjoyed so much had caused a complete change in the seascape. Most of the icebergs had melted and the few that remained were small and unimpressive.

We got back to Anchorage in time for a little rest and recreation. Deborah picked me up at nine-thirty and we picked up her mother, Jackie, at the airport. We yakked like magpies all the way home. Deborah kissed her mother and left. I guess she knew what was coming and wasn't up to it.

Robin, Alex, Jackie and myself drank wine and talked until about two in the morning and by six that morning I knew that the day would be a total wipeout, migraine headache and all.

By noon everything was under control and the headache was gone. I took the van in for an oil change. That afternoon we met a few more of Jackie's family members and enjoyed a steak, potato, mushroom and salad dinner washed down with lots of wine and German chocolate cake for dessert. We all went to bed early.

We enjoyed one last coffee with Jackie and were back on the road again.

Chapter Forty-two

Beautiful Downtown Talkeetna

During our getaway coffee Jackie mentioned that "if she had a significant other she would have preferred living in Talkeetna than Anchorage." When we saw the sign we knew that we had to take the fourteen-mile trek off the highway to see it.

"We must have heard wrong," I said to Alex as we drove into town. "No one in their right mind would come to this place voluntarily."

We parked right in front of the "Welcome to Beautiful Downtown Talkeetna" sign located in the park just as we entered. The old-fashioned main street through the town was the only paved road. Log cabins and clapboard houses and businesses lined the street and ended at the Susitna River. We walked all the roads including some of the out of the way side streets and although we found a delightful friendliness in all the people we passed I could not imagine Jackie saying that she would actually move there if she had her way.

We stopped into the Talkeetna Roadhouse, Talkeetna's oldest restaurant and lodge, for a drink and since it felt like a mini-museum with memorabilia hanging everywhere, we looked around and talked to the owners awhile. They shared with us some of the experiences with the local, colorful customers, a bit of the history of the area and what we had left to see before moving on. We listened intently and took it all in. It sure was friendly.....but live there?.....I don't think so.

By the time we found ourselves driving the fourteen miles back out to the main road a couple of hours had evaporated. There were several cars, vans and motorhomes stopped at a lookout point. We stopped to find out what they were looking at. They were pointing at the sky. We looked and saw nothing but clouds but we pointed along with them anyway. We thought we were the brunt of some asinine joke until some of the clouds cleared away and discovered that what we were actually seeing was the peak of Mt. McKinley. We thought it was all cloud. We realized that it was all snow-covered Mt. McKinley. We stood and stared in awe. We stayed for a long time and did not bother with pictures. There was no way we would be able to distinguish the clouds from the peak in a four-by-six inch glossy.

We enjoyed a peaceful lunch amongst the trees in a park close to the sighting. Within a half-hour we were back on the road. We were about half way to Denali when an ear-splitting beep, that damn near scared me out of a year's growth, reverberated inside my van. The oil light suddenly flashed bright red and stayed glowing. I pulled off to the side of the road immediately. I turned off the engine; my heart pounding in my ears.

Alex was the first one out of the van. He checked the undercarriage for a black, gooey puddle or any other sign of a leak. There was nothing. He checked the oil with the dipstick and it was right where it was supposed to be. He found the manual in the glove compartment and discovered that it beeped when it was lonely and wanted to be manhandled.....or something equally as stupid. After checking everything we could and found absolutely nothing wrong, I restarted the engine. We drove away like nothing significant had occurred.

We drove directly to Denali to see what was available in the way of camping spots and tours. The campground was full. We booked a park tour for the next day and left to find a campground with an available camping site. For the next few days we camped at Denali Grizzly Bear Cabins and Campground.

We arrived back at Denali National Park and Preserve early the next morning. The eleven o'clock ranger program was about wolves. The ranger got all the kids up on the stage howling and rolling around like wolves and their cubs. It was very cute.

The twelve o'clock program was a slide presentation about the park and that was magnificent since it showed flowers, animals and the mountain up close and personal and at its best.

After lunch in the van we boarded the bus for our eight-hour tour of Denali. Vehicles are no longer permitted beyond fourteen miles into the park and we were all looking forward to being able to do some sightseeing without driving. The bus took us as far as the Eiselson Visitor Center.

We saw caribou and grizzly bears so close that the pictures I took will remain a treasured keepsake. We caught a glimpse of a moose and her baby as they headed back into the heavy brush. We also stopped for another peek at the peak and were told that the zenith of Mt. McKinley is visible only a few days of the year. The entire trip would have been a "once in a lifetime" affair had it not been for some bratty kid that sat (jumped, rocked, bounced, kicked, bellowed and poked) beside me for eight hours and made my life a living hell. Had there been another vacant seat I surely would have changed but no one, even his mother who had a smaller version of the horror sitting on her lap, wanted to change seats with me. Perhaps next time I'll opt for traveling as a hood ornament. I'm sure the trip would have been far more pleasant, even having to pick the bugs out of my teeth.

We arrived back at the campground around eight. I took a long, warm, rejuvenating shower hoping to wash away even the memory of those sticky little fingers. We had a quick, scrambled egg dinner around nine and retired for the night, totally exhausted, long before the sun went down.

Chapter Forty-three

Mush I Tell You

The next day was pure joy and remains, to this very minute, one of the highlights of my northern adventure. After a large, hearty breakfast we went off to visit the Denali Park Hotel to spend a bit of time walking around the gift shop, the snack shop, the Railcar Lounge and the outside grounds. Late morning we went to the auditorium in the hotel for a program on Denali trivia.

Early afternoon we had a two-mile trek on a well-worn path to the dog sled kennels. We stopped for a picnic lunch on route and still arrived before the tour started. We had several minutes to play with the pups that just begged to be picked up. They were so cuddly but squirmed until you put them down. Once down they begged to be picked up again.

The adult dogs were inside one huge compound and each dog was roped to its own house. They were silent. All the adults were either sleeping on top of their house or lolling around on the ground. They paid no mind whatsoever to the people roaming around waiting to pet them. They were totally indifferent.

When the busload of people arrived it was time for the dogs to go to work and didn't they know it! As soon as the sled was brought out the howling started. They started barking nonstop and jumping up and down, sideways and in circles in the hope of being selected. These animals were eager.

The sled was put in place and chained to a hook that had been pounded into the ground. The equipment lay along the ground waiting for each dog to be harnessed into place. Each dog was selected individually and looked nothing like the purebred husky or malamute that I had become accustomed to in movies. There wasn't one dog that even came close to resembling Skeena, the Alaskan malamute that I owned for years.

The ranger walked the dog on his back legs to the place where he was strapped into the harness. It looked strange, almost like the ranger was strangling the animal. It was later explained that as soon as all four paws touched the ground they were off and running. They could easily, and they repeated easily, drag the ranger along the ground until he was forced to release the harness and the dog would be off on the one thousand one hundred fifty mile Iditarod solo. These were all powerful, eager working dogs and born to run.

Once all the dogs were harnessed into place the sled was released. The dogs, with the ranger guiding the sled, shot out like a bullet and the team was around the course in less than a minute. It was a fabulous demonstration, if you didn't blink and miss the whole thing. A short presentation followed with all of our questions answered.

We hiked back to the Visitor's Center. I should add that walking was not a prerequisite. We could have hopped onto the bus with the rest of the tourists but it was such a beautiful area to be hiking in and checking out the woodsy flora and fauna. Besides we needed the exercise and, for the moment, there wasn't a hint of a rain cloud.

After a quick dinner at the campground we went back to the Visitor's Center for the evening program with the ranger.

We thoroughly enjoyed a movie and discussion about the Alaska Sled Dog and the second movie, on Denali's Changing Seasons, rounded out our long day very nicely.

It was there that we learned that there are four seasons in the north country. They consist of June, July, August and winter.

Chapter Forty-four

A Mud Bath

The drive to Fairbanks the next day was pleasant, uneventful and without much to see along the way. Besides it would have been difficult to surpass the splendor of Denali. We found our campground just off one of the main streets. Alex and Robin set up the tenting material, while I made a list of the things we needed, and within ten minutes were on our way to the heart of Fairbanks for some grocery shopping.

After restocking the larder we went to the University of Alaska and their experimental flower, herb and vegetable garden. With such long summer days and lots (too much for our liking) of rain things grow quickly and much larger than in the lower forty-eight. From the vegetable garden we walked to the next area where these huge vegetables were being consumed.....at the experimental pig farm. It was a large, grassy area where the pigs could roam freely but each animal had his or her own home. Some of them sat in the doorway looking out at the rest of the world, appearing very much like a dog waiting for his master to come get him. A few seemed to enjoy the mud bath located at the bottom of the hill close to the fencing. Having wallowed in a mud bath myself I know how good they felt.

That night we had hamburgers on the barbecue but the mosquitoes and gnats drove us inside. This was the first time in a long time that I was able to pop the top on the camper. It looked and felt positively palatial. It was finally warm enough and there was no rain in the forecast, but, of course, that meant very little. For the moment, we were enjoying it.

We found the museum early the next morning and although I really enjoyed seeing the remains of Blue Babe, a thirty-six thousand-year-old bull, the museums were starting to run together. There were more presentations on wolves, moose and bear, all of which we had seen in movies, on posters, stuffed and, of course, in the wild.

If you are a fisherman or a hunter or would prefer to live as a recluse Alaska is a paradise. If you want to test your mettle Alaska is the place to do it; however, I'm not a fisherman, nor a hunter and I would prefer camping right in downtown Toronto, Boston or San Francisco than in some off the beaten track woodsy setting. My mettle, on this trip, had been tested far more aggressively than I wanted to admit. It was in Fairbanks that I was starting to long for some civilization, some warmth, perhaps a bath, perhaps someone different to talk to. I wanted.....I don't know what exactly.....I just wanted!

I felt a little better the next day. I figured that the only way I was going to be able to stop running around for a while was to complete my tour of Alaska. I was determined to enjoy the last of the adventure no matter what reared its ugly head.

Fairbanks was more interesting than most of the cities. We found the Land Management Office and spent the afternoon enjoying some different films. One was on the Glacier Bay glaciers and the other on Jay Hammond's (the former governor of Alaska) people of Alaska. Both were far more informative than the ones on animals and thanks to Alex's request we even saw a couple of cartoons that were made in Alaska.

ALASKA BOUND *and Gagged*

We walked the downtown area. We went into some jewelry stores and found artisans working with gold nuggets, crafting them into fine jewelry. A nugget, we discovered, is a rather klunky-looking stone so it is hard to work with in its natural state. They didn't seem to mind the fact that we were watching them work so we stayed.

For the afternoon we went to Alaskaland. It is normally a theme park but that part of it was closed for the season and there was very little else going on. We did go into all the little craft shops and mini-museums and jewelry shops that were open but there were no other tourists around so it looked rather vacant and bleak and forlorn.

The last shop we walked into we were greeted by a giant Kodiak bear rearing up on his hind legs, his front paws reaching up to grab us. He was stuffed, of course, but no less impressive. The woman behind the cash shivered and said "close that door. It's cold out there. I think I'll go home and curl up with bear."

"Excuse me," I said.

She repeated, "I think I'll go home and curl up with the bear."

"I drove here from Sarasota, Florida," I advised her. "Florida has eight women to every man. Oprah Winfrey told us that for every woman in Alaska there are approximately thirty men. And you want to go home to curl up with a bear?"

"Well," she said very seriously belying the twinkle in her eye, "if your looking for a man in Alaska the odds are very, very good. But the goods are very, very odd."

She was so right. From what I had seen of the place.....the clerk, one. Oprah, nothing.

Alaskaland is also the favorite spot of the "all you can eat" salmon bake but we all had the feeling that our "all you can eat" days were over. We would have had to eat sitting on outside benches and it was too cold. We would have been the only ones stuffing ourselves and it just didn't seem like fun.

The date was August nineteenth and winter was fast approaching. We were told that the first snowfall could come at anytime. Without sun, a brisk wind and clouds forming that snowfall could have buried us during the night. Fortunately it didn't.

We left early the next morning. Our first stop just outside Fairbanks was the North Pole. We had to stop and say "hello" to Santa. He is a year-round resident; however, I was sure he was not going to visit me this year.

I walked over to get a candy cane and to take some pictures. I explained to Santa that I had been good all year although not necessarily by choice but before he would give me a candy cane, the dirty old man insisted that I sit on his lap. I got my candy cane. I had some pictures taken and hopefully gave him a hernia. He'll know better next time.

The store was fun and well presented and since there was nothing left to see in the North Pole we headed south. We stopped in Delta Junction, the official end of the Alaska Highway. It was milepost one thousand, four hundred and twenty-two. We got our certificates stating that we had traveled the entire length of the Alaska Highway, took pictures at the post marker, just as I had done at milepost zero in Dawson Creek and we were gone like a shot.

Except for seeing moose on the road, that was gone before you could blink an eye, the ride was uneventful. The leaves on the trees were either changing colors or brown and dead, clinging to the limb with a last drop of energy. We arrived back into familiar territory. We camped in Tok.

Tok is the only city that we had to pass through twice. Once on the way in before heading south to do the complete circle and arriving back in Tok from the north. A few miles south of Tok we would get on the Taylor Highway. Maybe.

Chapter Forty-five

The Top of the World

The campground in Tok was almost empty. Amongst all the other problems I was starting to feel uncomfortable about the fact that I were still that far north. That fact did not seem to bother my companions. Nights were getting down to freezing and we still had over a week in this neck of the woods AND I still had the Taylor Highway to contend with.

I had heard so many nightmarish stories about the Taylor Highway that I was intimidated before I started. I promised myself that if it so much as sprinkled I would bypass that road and leave the Top of the World Highway and the most charming city in all of the north country, Dawson City, for some other trip.

We had intermittent sun and cloud when we started out. I really felt that I wanted to see it all. I knew in my gut that this would be my first and last trip to the land of the midnight sun and I didn't want to have to come back because I had skipped a spot or two that everyone talked about as being fantastic. The whole state was just too big and far too intimidating for my liking. It was all just scenery. If I saw what I wanted to the first time around there would be no reason to come back. The people were Americans. The food was just plain, ordinary food. It was stuff you could get anywhere except, of course, for the moose meat, reindeer bratwurst and salmon that jumped right out of the water and onto your barbecue. The museums were few and far between. The weather was lousy and would only get worse. The rest was all just scenery.

When I turned onto the Taylor Highway, just south of Tok, the weather was clear. We came across a bit of gravel here and a pothole there but nothing that I couldn't handle. In the blink of an eye all of that changed.

The rain two days before had turned this section to mud. The soft shoulder bordered a precipice and I knew it would be deadly to get too close. I stayed in the center of the road. My van started sliding sideways in the muck. I dared not stop. I couldn't back up because there was traffic behind me. I could only inch my way forward in the hope of finding someplace to turn around. I wanted out.

Alex offered to drive but I knew that he would not always be around and stupidly I felt I had to get through this myself. After about the third or fourth offer I screamed that I would handle it. He backed off. We said nothing for a long time and I slowly willed my blood pressure to dip below three hundred. I felt like I was about to explode.

The slalom course was twenty-three miles long. During the three hours that it took me to drive this hellish section of what is loosely called the Taylor HIGHWAY I cursed and swore and prayed a lot with only one funny incident to break the tension. It was a simple yellow-and-black construction sign that had been strategically placed by the side of the road. It said "BUMP."

I could finally breathe a little easier when I got through that muck section but I still had a long way to go on a gravel road. I was afraid to go any faster because I never knew when a frost heave or a break in the road would be just around the bend. We were still traveling at about twenty-five miles an hour heading for an old wooden bridge when we saw it. I had just completed twenty-three miles of the most horrendous and terrifying road conditions you could imagine without a hint of a sign and there it was.....BUMP. My little van had taken such a severe beating I don't think it felt it. I know we didn't.

Storms start and stop with amazing speed and since Chicken, Alaska, population thirty-seven, was one of the two towns on the one hundred and eighty mile stretch of road we decided to wait out the storm and have lunch. The rain stopped before lunch was over and we were able to open the door and let some of the body heat out. We enjoyed the mini-tour since there wasn't much else to see.

The town consisted of an Emporium, a bar and restaurant, one shop, two outhouses and a couple of gasoline pumps. The post office, one of the most popular in Alaska was not visible from the road. We purchased some postcards showing the entire downtown of Chicken, outhouses and all, wrote a few simple messages and addressed them. Before leaving town we found the post office out in the suburbs and mailed our cards. We also found the private road that lead to the homes of the thirty-seven people that occupied the town. It was a gated community or a least a chained community complete with padlock. Tourists were not permitted.

On our way out of town we stopped to pan for gold. Yes it was still drizzling and the water was a degree or two above freezing but we did it anyway. We didn't last long. Bear in mind that I spend my winters in Florida and my companions were from Georgia. Ice cold water is supposed to have bourbon or a sprig of mint in it or something equally as refreshing.

For your information only, an interesting bit of trivia about the name of the town, Chicken. The local folk had actually decided to name to place Ptarmigan, after the state bird;

however no one knew how to spell it and decided that since it looked like a chicken anyway.....need I say more.

The second town on this road is Poker Creek, population two. This is the most northerly land border crossing in America. This is where Canada meets the United States. This is also where the Taylor Highway meets the Top of the World Highway. This is also where one house stood right across the street from the Customs Office. This was all there was in Poker Creek.

Can you imagine the housing shortage I would create had I chosen to make my home in Poker Creek? Would it be feasible to build a supermarket, a theater, a bowling alley and a library for just three of us.....and who would I date. Bad enough that I felt like a third wheel everywhere else. This would be a third wheel forever. I decided to forget it. We crossed the border back into Canada.

This was the Top of the World Highway and, of that, there was absolutely no doubt. We were above the tree line. It was a sheer cliff on both sides and we could see the tops of mountains a hundred miles in every direction. There was an incredible feeling of exhilaration that I certainly never experienced before and could not imagine ever feeling again. This was vastness beyond imagination. It was certainly the Top of the World.

The road conditions on the Canadian side were not much better. I still drove slowly so we could look around and enjoy the vista and once it dawned on me that a breakdown on these roads would spell disaster I concentrated on getting to Dawson City. The intimidation had returned.

There was very little traffic on the road and we had no trouble making it to the Yukon River, where a ferry waited to take the cars across to Dawson City. I wanted to kiss the ground when we arrived at the campground.

The entire trip had taken eight hours. We had traveled a total of one hundred and eighty miles. This was the first time all day that I could breathe a sigh of relief. It was after seven in the evening when we arrived. After setting up in our spot we treated ourselves to dinner out.

Chapter Forty-six

Dawson City

Dawson City was a breath of fresh air.....cold but fresh. There was definitely enough going on to stay active on our last few days. We could spend several days checking out all the touristy places without running out of things to do or see. We could also walk the town instead of driving.

Our first order of business after setting up camp and getting a delicious roast chicken dinner at a small, local restaurant just around the corner from the campground, was to learn a little about the history of the city. We took our guidebooks out to dinner with us.

During the height of the Gold Rush, Dawson City had the largest population west of Winnipeg and north of San Francisco. There were approximately thirty thousand people. That number has been reduced to three hundred and fifty year round residents. It is the most charming city of the entire northland. The streets are not only "not paved with gold".....they are not paved at all. Wooden sidewalks are still maintained and felt soft and spongy under the sandals that I now wore with thick woolly socks.

Bright and early the next morning, after a quick breakfast, we headed downtown to the Visitor's Center. We watched a couple of movies of Dawson City in the good old days. We also took an extensive tour of the Palace Grand Theater. The theater was built in 1899 and had been recently reconstructed to its original grandeur. The only major change made was from gaslight to electric light and the show, the Gaslight Follies, that we saw, or should I say, we participated in, was enormously entertaining.

In the 1900's it was customary for the ladies and their husbands to sit on the second level balcony. If they had a new hat or dress on they would hang over the balcony so the world would be able to see them. Only on a rare occasion did madam hang so far over the ledge that she fell to the floor below landing on the riffraff. Only the men occupied the downstairs and the bald men usually sat in front so they could get their heads kissed when the ladies of the performance came down from the stage into the audience.

On that first afternoon we visited the museum and toured Jack London's house. He had spent a few years panning for gold. He never struck it rich except in gathering material for his books and stories.

From Jack London's home we walked just a few houses over to Robert Service's home. We listened to an actor, Robert Daly, recite Service's poems for almost two hours. He was dressed in costume and recited the poems from memory stopping only occasionally to glimpse at the sky or take a drink of water. No one moved except to laugh. No one asked questions.

After the poetry reading we spent hours wandering all the back streets of Dawson. A little game we played was to try and find one windshield that did not have a crack or a hole in it. We didn't find even one, not even mine, but we did end up seeing some unique homes. A few were right out of Better Homes and Gardens and, unfortunately for the owners, were standing next to houses that should have been out in the woods someplace perhaps with a little half moon carved into the door. Our final destination for the afternoon was the cemetery. There was much to learn visiting gravesides and here we learned that nothing stayed buried too long. Everything moved and tilted and shifted thanks to permafrost. The entire graveyard looked like it was out of a Frankenstein movie. Faithful servant Igor had left unkempt mounds of earth after running off with the contents of several caskets. It was easy for my imagination to run wild. We didn't stay long but managed a look at every headstone whether they were legible or not.

After dinner we went back to the museum to hear Sally Wilson speak of her thirteen years in the bush. She and her husband built boats, mushed dogs, tobogganed and snow-shoed between Dawson City and Whitehorse on a regular basis. All of their escapades had been turned into best selling books. They were still living the adventure together and loving every minute of Arctic life. She was the spokesperson. They both answered questions. The questions went on forever. A few purchased autographed copies of their books. We did not.

The evening ended at the only gambling hall in all of Canada, Diamond Tooth Gertie's. One entrance fee got us into the building, supposedly to gamble. Once inside we could watch all or any of the three nightly shows featuring Gertie herself who is billed as "a more popular attraction then Dredge No. 4." She had the voice of a songbird, easy on the ears. She crooned to some poor schnook in the audience while sitting on his lap and stroking his bald head until he threatened to crawl under the table. He was from a small town in Saskatchewan.

She milled about the tables talking to visitors, finding out where people were from and telling one-line jokes in between the songs. We whooped-and-hollered with everyone else when the can-can dancers, dressed in either emerald green, ruby red or royal blue gay nineties costumes, kicked their way onto the stage.

We stayed through two of the shows, each with different players, except for Gertie, of course. We would have stayed for the third show but it had been a super-full day and our beds were enticing us with lullabies whispered in our ears. A great time was had by all. We walked back to the campground.

It didn't take long the following morning to find our way to Dredge No. 4. Even though people are still making a living panning for gold Dredge No. 4 was the last of its kind in the north country. It would still be in operation today if heavy rains had not lifted it and tipped it on its side in the 1970's. It was righted in 1992, anchored and currently in the process of being restored. For the moment it is used only as a tourist attraction. The tour took the entire morning and the cool outside temperature made our stay a little uncomfortable. Once inside the building it was extremely damp and musty. An informative and interesting morning, but very uncomfortable.

Just as we were heading back to Dawson the sun peeked out from behind the clouds. We were very grateful for the bit of warmth it provided. After lunch we toured the Northwest Mounted Police building and the Commissioner's house. We took a tour of Dawson City with a young historian named Carrie. She was the first person we met who was actually born in the Yukon so we trusted that her information was accurate. She filled us in on other bits and pieces of information since her father supported the family by gold mining.

It was also interesting to see and take pictures of buildings that were no longer in use because of permafrost. Carrie explained that as soon as anything is built on top of permafrost it starts to defrost causing the earth to heave in all directions. It upsets whatever is built on it, causing some structures to lean in and some to lean out. It does wonders to the landscape.

That evening we went to the Gaslight Follies. That was a real hoot.....lots of great belly-laughs. Some of the people chosen out of the audience were as funny as the performers themselves. One lady started ad-libbing and the cast member played along and let her be the funny one. She kept gesturing to her husband to get some pictures taken but he couldn't seem to understand what she wanted. The audience loved it and everyone, except him, snapped a bunch of pictures.

It was another long, fast paced day filled with amusing people, unusual places and unique things to see.

The Arctic is definitely a place of dreams, or in some cases, nightmares. No one leaves the north untouched. It is still a wild and untamed land and a land that must be respected or you die. Dawson City was the only place that I could visualize myself spending a winter.....and I certainly did not visualize it for long. Day by day we could see the changes in the air. The mornings were cold and foggy and it was taking hours for the sun to break through the fog.

At eight-fifteen on our last morning we were waiting in line at Bear Creek. This was where the gold was weighed and measured and sent on to Ottawa, Canada's capital. The tour was conducted by Carrie and was as interesting as our last tour with her.

From Bear Creek we were back on the road and on our way south to Whitehorse. Except for the tawny-colored lynx that wandered onto the road and stopped to stare at us as we approached, the trip was uneventful. I slowed the van in the hopes that we could inch our way up and not scare the animal but that didn't work. He stopped, looked at us and was on his way before we could really make our move. He was beautiful.

Chapter Forty-seven

Stubborn as a Mule

It was a long drive back to Whitehorse. There was little color left on the trees and dead leaves were blowing all over the road or mounding into heaps by the side. We got caught up in more construction and my windshield sustained a few more direct hits. I was surprised that none of the chips or cracks had spread beyond a millimeter or two. With every hit I expected my windshield to become a living spider web being woven before my eyes.

During one section of the construction I was riding down the center of the road like everyone else and a ridge of pilings had slowly built up under my van. The pilings were getting higher and I could hear the scraping on the underbelly of the van. I started to panic as I tried to drive through them. Without Alex's assistance I would have panicked out of control.

"Slow down," he said firmly but calmly as the dirt and pebbles crackled under the wheels and peppered the bottom of the van. "Take your foot off the gas and slow down.....now!"

Without jamming on the brakes, as I was so tempted to do, I took my foot off the gas pedal, as he instructed. I tapped the brake and released it several times. I slowed almost to a stop and was finally able to steer over what had become a dirt path down the center of the road. I was really on edge but I

ALASKA BOUND *and Gagged*

drove for another couple of hours just to say "I did it" and then turned the driving (gladly) over to Alex who confidently got us to Whitehorse in one piece.

The drive from Dawson to Whitehorse was three hundred and sixty miles. That was enough for one day, especially with the bad section of the road we had encountered. Even with good roads it would have been enough. We enjoyed a pizza and salad for dinner.

While I stayed at the same campground in the heart of Whitehorse (and right next door to the Pizza Hut) that I had camped in during my earlier visit, the Sawatsky's decided to treat themselves to a night in a local motel. We were all ready for a bit of luxury. Theirs came a little earlier than mine.

It was a lucky move on their part. Just as I dropped them off with all their paraphernalia the rain started. It was icy cold and pummeled my windshield with pellets that melted the instant they hit.

When I returned to the campground another Westphalia, a model a few years older than mine had pulled into the adjacent spot. I knocked on their door since I couldn't resist saying hello to people from what I considered 'my neck of the woods'. Even though the license plates were from Ontario my neighbors were from two small cities in Quebec. Marie was from Chicoutimi and Jean Pierre was from Jonquire. For those of you who do not have any special fondness for the people of Quebec I should say, in their defense, that the natives from the smaller communities are warm, friendly and most hospitable and these two were no exception. I couldn't believe that they were just starting on their trek north. They were having some van troubles that were to be taken care of the next day and they would be on their way to Dawson City.

We talked most of the evening and when I brought out the wine jug, which I always kept full, the conversation became

171

even livelier. By the time we said our good nights in the wee hours of the morning I knew that I would sleep really, really well. The tension from the day's driving had left me completely, as did my ability to speak properly and focus my eyes. I took a couple of my favorite painkillers before retiring.

I awoke refreshed and delighted to be back in what appeared to be civilization. I also had a story idea and used my first three waking hours to get it down in my computer and printed out. I entitled it The Alaska Highway. When my friends arrived I read it to them. They seemed to enjoy it since they were part of it.

We spent the day walking Whitehorse and collecting the rest of the stamps that we needed for the Yukon passport that we had received at the Visitor's Center in Watson Lake. With ten stamps we would each be receiving a Yukon poster and our names would be put into a drum for a drawing of a gold nugget.

I visited the offices of the CBC (Canadian Broadcasting Company) and had them send e-mail to Michel Normand, the man from whom I had purchased the van. I wanted him to know that his little van had made it to parts of the world that he never even dreamed about.

We were on the last leg of our journey and the van started with an odd little, underlying 'thunk'. I knew it must be my imagination because it started so easily and stayed running so I said nothing. We stopped at the Visitor's Center and Transportation Museum just outside of town, got two more stamps in our passport and picked up our posters at the same time. Again there was that soft "thunk" when it started. I mentioned it to Alex. He heard nothing. We drove out.

Chapter Forty-eight

Dead as a Doornail

The journey to Skagway was uneventful and we camped in the same spot as before. From our vantage point we could watch as the ferries and cruise ships came in and went out. The trains were still taking people up the forty mile Klondike Gold Rush Trail and we still waved to them as they went by. They still waved back.

We walked the whole town one last time to see if there was anything new to see and our neighbors at the campground invited us to a "beach party" at one of the local bars. I have no idea where they found so much sand for the floor but the music was loud, the beer was cold and served by the pitcher and the dance floor was crowded. It was a terrific way to spend one of my last days on solid ground in the state known as The Last Frontier.

The following morning the van started with a 'thunk and a whistle'. Talk about not being a happy camper at that moment. We had one more day before sailing. I had to make it onto that ship with my belongings. I spent the day removing the bike rack and hoping the rack and the bicycle would fit inside the van. With the rack on the back the van was a foot and a half longer and would cost over a hundred dollars more because the overall length would fall into another category.

Joei Carlton Hossack

I had trouble falling asleep. I tossed and turned when I finally did manage to fall asleep, I couldn't stay asleep. The sailing was early and the morning tasks were overwhelming.

An overnight storm and ferocious winds kept us awake most of the time anyway. We had no trouble getting up and out early. We were all anxious to get away. We dressed quickly and with much difficulty loaded the van. It all fit but not without lots of shuffling, reorganizing and stuffing.

I got behind the wheel and turned the key. It was as dead as a doornail. Nothing! Not a sound! Alex got behind the wheel. Robin and I pushed the camper out onto the road that circled the campground. It started and died. We tried again. When the van started and moved under its own steam I motioned for Alex to keep moving. He drove it to the dock. Robin and I walked the short distance. Alex kept the motor going for a while. As I walked around the van I noticed that something was leaking. It wasn't oil. We weren't sure what it was. The longer it idled the more it dripped. Alex turned off the motor. I could do nothing but curse and swear.....and pray silently for divine intervention. I think we all did that.

I told the officials in the office my problem. I worried that they wouldn't let me on board with a vehicle that wasn't running. I would be up the proverbial creek without a paddle if that occurred. I was relieved when a couple of the big, burly guys said they would help in pushing the van if it became necessary.

When it was time to get on board the van started with no problem. I drove it into position and they placed rags under the van so whatever was leaking wouldn't run all over the place. Once the motor was turned off the leaking stopped. I checked it periodically during the trip. The underneath stayed dry. Thank God for small mercies.

ALASKA BOUND *and Gagged*

I was relieved to be on board with my vehicle. I didn't have to drive anywhere. Knowing that I didn't have to drive anywhere for a few days I became positively giggly. They had a full schedule of events on board. I attended lectures. I attended movies. Rangers with the National Park Service did a great job of conducting the lively discussions.

"Do any of the passengers ever give lectures?" I asked rather coyly.

"What do you want to talk about?" the young ranger asked, his eyes beaming with enthusiasm.

I backed down immediately and realized that would be a terrific way to travel and get my traveling expenses paid; however, not on this trip. I knew that it was definitely something I wanted to look into for the future.

I attended every lecture, even the ones that didn't sound too interesting, just to keep my mind off my problems. There was one on Alaska trivia. Another on the inland ferry route, towns along the way and another on what the waters contain. They gave a lecture on almost everything you could imagine and were wonderful about answering questions. When they didn't have the answers off-hand they quickly found out and came back with a full report.

My first day on board I met a couple from Bozeman, Montana, a favorite stopping ground for me. Virginia and Al were interesting to talk to and, when I became a little sad talking about my husband, Virginia was kind enough to let me pour my heart out to her. Her only comment was that at one time or another we all have tragedies in our lives. She just let me bend her ear.

The following morning more than half the passengers lined the side of the boat as we watched a couple of humpback whales breach the water within picture-taking range. A few dolphins played in the surf left by the ferry. They skimmed the top of the water, jumping when they felt the urge, and followed alongside. It felt like being back in Florida. This was our mid-morning entertainment.

That day it was my turn to listen. I met Gus. He had been divorced about ten years and for the last two years he had been living like a recluse on one of the islands before heading into the big city of Skagway to catch the ferry.

"As it happens," he said, "when you spend too much time alone, strange things happen. I had a vision of an old sweetheart. She came to me in a dream. It was so powerful that I had to find out what happened to her."

He took a chance and tried to locate her through her parents who still lived in the same town in Michigan where they all grew up.

"Her parents told me that Margaret had been widowed several years before and had just completed a two year stint teaching English in Ankara, Turkey. She was on her way home to Michigan. I left my name, address and phone number and I knew she would call. I had many sleepless weeks before that call came," he confessed.

During the next three months they corresponded by mail and by phone. Gus was heading south because they were going to meet for the first time in forty years.

I spent hours listening to Gus, not offering any advice but totally engrossed in the story. He had no expectations he said, "but a friendship would be nice. I expect no more than that. Anything more would be a bonus."

He promised he would let me know what happened. I never heard from him again. I hope with all my heart that things worked out for my friend Gus and his globetrotting Margaret. Even a friendship would be nice.

We stopped in Alaska's capital, Juneau, just long enough to get off the ship and wander around the harbor but not long enough to go into town for a visit. Even by taxi there would not have been enough time to see the Capital Buildings let alone the city itself.

Chapter Forty-nine

Ketchikan

There was a stop in Sitka to pick up or let off passengers but it was the middle of the night and I never knew what happened except to be groggily aware that the engine noise had stopped and started. I had no idea what happened or at what time.

Before our eight-hour stop in Ketchikan I again ran into some old friends on board. Even though they were sound asleep on two couches in the lounge I recognized Michael and Chris, my school teacher friends on sabbatical, with the blue Volkswagen Westphalia and Ontario license plates. Hours later I ran into them on an outside deck. They had gotten on the ferry in the middle of the night after a brief stop in Wrangell, another stop that I wasn't even aware of, and were sailing to Ketchikan. I told them about my van problems and Michael gave me some toll-free telephone numbers to use and assured me that VW had guaranteed emergency towing service. I was relieved.

Before getting off the ship in Ketchikan I checked my VW dealer book and was thrilled to find a full-service one listed in Prince Rupert. I found a pay phone in the harbor, called and relayed my problems to the service manager. He assured me that I would be his first customer the next day and if I couldn't get to them they would arrange to have the van towed. For the first time in several days I felt the tension ease a bit. I could now fully enjoy my eight-hour stopover in Ketchikan.

Once away from the dock area where old warehouses and rundown properties lined the street, a part of town we would not normally call the scenic route, the landscape improved immensely. We walked along the waterfront and thoroughly enjoyed the view. Every property en route seemed to have either a boat or a seaplane in the water. When we arrived at the outskirts we discovered that Ketchikan was a beautiful, hilly walking town. It was interesting seeing the cruise ship dock as compared to the ferry dock. From the ferry dock we had a-mile-and-a-half to two-mile walk to the town. If you fell off the cruise ship, however, you landed either in a high-class restaurant or a high-class gift shop depending on whether you fell off the port or starboard side.

Since Ketchikan is five miles long and only four blocks wide we had no trouble covering the entire downtown area. We concentrated on the Totem Heritage Center. They had over thirty totem poles and fragments that had been retrieved from deserted Tlingit and Haida Indian villages. Some of the totem poles were over a hundred years old and had been beautifully preserved. Touching was not permitted. Even flash film would inflict damaged so that too was prohibited.

We wandered into the former "red light" district. Creek Street, as it is called, is a wooden street on pilings and begins just past the bridge. Black Mary, Dolly, Frenchie and others plied their trade for over half a century until 1954. Many of the homes and businesses have been restored, some turned into art and gift shops. Dolly's House, a former brothel, was open to the public but crowded so we didn't go in.

Except for the few museums, the interesting architecture in town and the rejuvenation of Creek Street, as with most towns on the water, they are shopping havens for the tourist.

Joei Carlton Hossack

After about five hours of touring with a stop for a fresh fish lunch and a beer we headed back to the ship. This was our last night in Alaska. It was so much warmer.

"It is so nice to be warm and in the sunshine for a change," I said to Robin.

"Be careful what you wish for," she answered.

Chapter Fifty

Pushed Off

I love being awakened in the middle of the night by several ear-splitting blasts from the ship's horn. It keeps me from wondering what I'm going to do with the rest of the day since I instantly go into cardiac arrest and have to worry if the paramedics are going to get to me in time.

We had arrived in Prince Rupert, British Columbia and after fumbling with clothes for the day and packing up my few toiletries I had to make my way down to where the vehicles were parked. Alex and Robin arrived within minutes after I did looking equally as disheveled.

I assumed that we would be allowed off first because we were first in line and all hands below deck were aware that we had problems. Needless to say the van didn't start and when everyone was sent off ahead of us we were pushed off onto the parking lot thanks to the help of a large crew.

This presented another problem. We had to keep the vehicle running while everyone went through customs. We were back on Canadian soil. Alex drove the van while I worried and watched the antifreeze, as I learned later, drip from the bottom.

When we got close to customs I had to get back behind the wheel. They would not look favorably on an American driver, not the owner, behind the wheel of a Canadian registered vehicle. Realizing our problem and having all the proper papers to show the agent we were ushered through quickly and efficiently. I drove the van to the Park Avenue campground while Alex and Robin walked the half-mile or so. With everything stuffed in the back and passenger seat there was no room for anything alive larger than a gerbil and even a gerbil would not have lasted long without his favorite wheel.

I found a spot, emptied the van of all of our belongings onto the grass while praying that the weather stayed warm and sunny. When Alex and Robin arrived we left Robin to set up their equipment while Alex and I drove to the VW dealer. Fortunately the van did not overheat on the short drive. We breathed a heavy sigh of relief to have made it to their parking lot. We arrived just as they were opening for the day.

It took no time at all to discover that the water pump was shot and since the van had an alarm system the alarm was malfunctioning and draining the battery. Unfortunately there was no time for a second opinion. We left the van, in what we hoped were capable hands, and walked back to get Robin and go out to breakfast.

Robin had set up their tenting equipment and all the goods and paraphernalia that I had left on the lawn was neatly tucked away inside the tent. We were ready for a little excursion. It was less than a block away that we sat down for a full-course breakfast, complete with bacon, eggs, hash brown potatoes, toast and coffee. We lingered over several cups of coffee knowing that we probably had all day to kill.

We walked much of Prince Rupert seeing many of the totem poles that were scattered throughout the city. We spent several hours at the museum and art gallery. We went out for a long, leisurely lunch. I managed to cash a check at the Royal Bank in downtown Prince Rupert and in an effort to keep busy spent the rest of the day wandering around totally aimlessly until exhaustion set in.

I returned to the garage rather late in the afternoon. The van was parked outside and (supposedly) ready to go. The service manager asked why the oil light stayed on when the van was turned on.

"It never did that before," I answered, clicking my tongue against the roof of my mouth letting him know that I was totally frustrated.

For the next two hours I waited while he checked the wiring. He said it was fixed and I was handed an itemized repair bill of over four hundred dollars.

Now if this were the end of the "repair" story I would have been thrilled to death. Read on.

I drove back to the campground. Alex and Robin were nowhere in sight. I crawled into the back and onto my bed and slept like a baby for hours. I awoke to a growling stomach ready to throw something together for dinner. We ate in almost total silence. We wandered around the campground. We met others that were staying for a day or two. The evening passed.

The next day was a test for the van and it passed with flying colors. Much of the drive was along the Skeena River. I had been so enamored with the name Skeena from years before that I had named our Alaska Malamute after the river. Much of the drive was done in silence. I just had the vision that Skeena was standing beside my late husband Paul. She had definitely been his dog. She only barely tolerated me.

We drove over three hundred miles that day. We camped at Burns Lake that night. It was a treat being back in the south. The weather was warm. It stayed sunny all day. My van seemed to be performing well. For the minute, all was right with the world.

Joei Carlton Hossack

The next day we drove a little over four hundred miles but it was imperative that we make it to a specific Cache Creek campground. I believe that I have already explained that I would drive a million miles if there was a hot tub at the end of it. I am so shallow but there you have it. I drove over four hundred miles so I could sit and soak in a hot tub for over two hours. It was worth every mile.

That night I thought I was calling the daughter of a friend living in Chilliwack, however it seems that my friends Beverley and Richard Hood, her parents, had arrived just a few minutes before the call. When Bev picked up the phone and heard my voice her first words were "you must have mental telepathy."

My heart jumped for joy when I heard that familiar voice. I loved knowing that they were looking forward to seeing me as much as I was looking forward to seeing them.

"I'll see you sometime tomorrow," I said after letting them know that I was relatively close by, or at least in the same province.

It was an amazing thing about my friends and family. It didn't seem to matter how much I enjoyed myself or how competent I was, no one wanted to see me wandering alone. The Hoods, and other acquaintances in the Westphalia club, had worried about me and, of course, close family members had been frantic when I hadn't written or called in a while. What was a short time for me had been endless worry to them. And it took me only fifty-one years to discover this. I must be growing up.

Chapter Fifty-one

The Hoods

It was sometime during our stop for lunch that I changed into shorts and discarded the heavy walking shoes I was wearing and slipped my sweaty feet into sandals without the heavy socks that I was so accustomed to wearing. I wiggled my toes that suddenly felt the same freedom that the rest of me felt. It was like crawling out of a cave into life-affirming sunshine.

Although the mileage on the map said one hundred and fifty I was not aware that one hundred of those miles would be over the Rockie's highest peaks and on a switch back road so narrow it was best suited for suicidal mountain goats or your run-of-the-mill Grande Prix driver behind the wheel of a Porsche. I guess that I was just anxious to get to Chilliwack and see my friends. I desperately wanted this part of the trip to be over.

The drive through the Fraser Canyon was breathtakingly beautiful and I slowed to watch the road and take in some of the spectacular scenery.

I called the Hoods immediately after checking into the campground. It was approximately two hours later than I had anticipated. No one was home.

Alex, Robin and I went out for a long walk and a large, all-dressed pizza. I called again just before we finished up our late lunch or an early dinner and was delighted when someone picked up the phone. That was around three o'clock. Robin and Alex preferred going back to the campground to make some phone calls about a car rental and to check on their goods that had been delivered to storage.

I waited in the parking lot and was so excited when I recognized Richard behind the wheel of a car. Beverley didn't even wait for it to come to a complete stop before she was out and hugging me. Beverley insisted that I sit in the front seat so I could see where we were going.

I couldn't wait to get my whole story out. Questions were being fired at me at the same rate that pebbles were fired at me during the road construction. The second I answered one I was bombarded with another.

That afternoon I met daughter Heather and son-in-law Sean. They felt that I hadn't driven enough or seen enough so that afternoon we visited Hope, British Columbia to see the chain saw carvings and then to the Coquilla Canyon to see the tunnels and to watch the salmon jump. We talked almost nonstop. It was just so great having someone different to talk to that I probably did more babbling than actually telling them about my Alaska experience. Richard and Beverley had lots of questions about the trip and they had promised the Westphalia club that they would report back to them so they needed specific answers to specific questions. The entire club was anxious to hear about my journey and to know that I was safe and sound.

That evening daughter Dianne, whom I was meeting for the first time, and son Chris, whom I had met in Ontario, came over for dinner. We had a rousing game of Trivial Pursuit, ladies against gentlemen. They weren't gentlemen.....ladies lost.

I arrived back at the campground late in the evening and crawled into my camper without disturbing the Sawatskys.

ALASKA BOUND *and Gagged*

Robin and Alex had taped a note to my door early the next morning saying that they had gone into Vancouver to rent a car and would see me later.

I'm sure they were as anxious to be on their own as I was to have them "be" on their own. Most of the trip had been terrific and I was certainly delighted to have had their company. I would have been far too intimidated to do all that driving alone in such a remote state but the last two or three weeks had become jaw-clenching tense. I knew more about them and they knew more about me then either one of us wanted to know about each other. When we started on the adventure in Whitehorse I don't think any of us realized how long six weeks was in real day-to-day, minute-by-minute living. We all needed our own space and were finally going to get it.

Robin and Alex were not back when the Hoods picked me at around one in the afternoon. I was told to bring my bathing suit. A cooler with picnic stuff and drinks was already in the trunk along with all kinds of junk food that I loved but rarely bought because I could rarely stop eating it. We drove out to Cultus Lake. I dipped my big toe in the water and everything up to my knee went numb.

"Hey," I yelled at Beverley, "if I had wanted this kind of ice water I would have stayed in Alaska. That's not a swimming platform out there, it's an iceberg that is nowhere close to melting."

I returned to the blanket for Freetos, chips, dip, soft drinks and conversation. We were back at Heather's apartment by late afternoon for a pizza and chicken wing dinner and a rematch of Trivial Pursuit. Lost again.

I had talked about my sister so much during the evening that they insisted I call her. I called collect. I had written often but I had not called since my excited call from Whitehorse and she had worried. She had her own news to relay.

Joei Carlton Hossack

Her job had come to an end. The building that she lived in had suffered severe damage during the 1994 earthquake and was being torn down. She and her husband were being evicted.

"Mona," I said trying to keep my voice from quivering, "I'll be there in a few days. I'll pick you up. You'll come with me to Florida and then to Canada. Don't move until I get there. I won't know where to find you." She assured me that she would be fine temporarily and would wait for me.

When I got off the phone I broke down into tears. Richard and Beverley and the rest of the family were there to comfort me. It was so hard to think or to talk after that so they let me cry it out. I knew most of it was just the tension of not talking to her in so many weeks. We normally talk every week or two. They drove me back to the campground when they knew I would be okay.

I was awake most of the night so I knew it was raining. The following morning I said my good byes to Alex and Robin and called the Hoods. I cleaned up the camper, did a bit of grocery shopping at a local market and headed for the border.

Chapter Fifty-two

On My Own at Last

I felt relieved to be back on the road by myself, even if my mission was not a happy one. It had been two years since I had seen my sister and although we talked for hours on the phone I missed her. I missed talking to her face to face.

It didn't take long to get to the border. It was there that I had my first laugh of the day. As a matter of fact it was my only laugh of the day.

"Where do you live?" he asked.

"Toronto." I answered.

"Where are you going?" he asked.

"To California," I answered, "to visit my sister."

"All alone?" he asked a little concerned.

I laughed and told him I had taken a little detour through the Yukon and Alaska and this was the easy part.

"What was it like?" he asked.

"The roads are incredibly shitty and so was the weather," I answered not really concerned about my choice of words.

"Have a good time," he said without even looking at my identification.

The rest of the trip for that day was uneventful. I checked into the River Oaks Park in Washington State and the woman at the desk gave me an extra ten-percent discount because I was alone. She also went out of her way to find me a cable hookup for my little black and white television set. I was most grateful. I felt very comfortable and secure in my spot even though the wind had picked up rather dramatically during the evening and threatened to blow me away.

The Oregon coast made for a lovely drive and I enjoyed all the little towns along the way. Normally I would have driven a very short distance and stopped for a picnic or a walk around town. I would have searched out an ice cream parlor or a fudge shop to get my daily sweet-tooth fix. I would have scoured the town for some out-of-the-way boutique or a gift shop selling local, hand crafted wares. I didn't do any of it. I just kept moving. Mona had told me that she would be okay for a couple of weeks but that did not ease my mind.

There are four of us in the family. We are by no means a closely-knit family especially with all of us living in different parts of Canada and the United States, but a crisis, however minor, is another matter. I would be there for Mona like my family was there for me in 1992 when my husband died in a German campground. I needed to see for myself that she was okay.

The Oregon coastline was magnificent but, like Alaska, had more than its share of rain. To give myself a little break during a downpour I stopped at the Bridge Interpretive Center in Alsea. I spent a small part of the day enjoying movies on the five different bridges that had been built down the coast. It sure beat standing out in the rain giving each bridge the once-over.

I fell in love with the Newport area and went for a long walk through town noticing the quaint little houses with lace curtains. I visited the few shops and sampled a sliver of homemade, pina colada fudge that was offered at the end of a Popsicle stick. To this day, just the mention of pina colada fudge and I become one of Pavlov's dogs. For that reason alone I could have stayed and made Newport my home but I thanked her, purchased a couple of post cards and went back to the van. I stopped at a rest area and filled out a few of the cards while having some lunch. It was there that I met John and Marge, a retired couple enjoying a leisurely lunch in the rest area/park/tourist information center. The lived full-time in their motorhome and I envied them. They were heading for a campground in Northern California where they would meet up with some friends for a month.

"We drive about seventy-five miles in a day and try to stay a week or so," Marge volunteered.

"Where are you going today?" I asked.

Marge mentioned a spot that I knew to be less than twenty miles down the road. She looked at me quizzically and said "seventy-five miles is not a hard and fast rule, you know."

Oh how I envied them at that moment and told them so. It had been a very long time since I had stopped for a week anywhere along my route and I had to admit that I was exhausted.....physically, emotionally and spiritually. I really needed to put my feet up on something that did not have wheels on it; however, it was still a long way from that day.

The spectacular scenery of the Oregon coast gave way to the Redwood Forest of Northern California. I had lived in the California from 1962 to 1971 and it had been so many years since I had visited that I had actually forgotten how beautiful it was. That night I camped about five miles north of Eureka, California.

I paid, parked, changed into my bathing suit and was in the hot tub before the cash register was closed. I soaked until a few of the aches and pains were gone. Since I was alone in the tub I only lasted a couple of hours. I tried calling my sister late in the afternoon but no one was home. There were very few people in the campground and it unnerved me walking around in the pitch dark with large trees that cast eerie shadows so I stayed in my camper that night.

I called early the next morning and spoke to my brother-in-law. I told him where I was and he laughed when I said, "Eureka, I have found it." I let him know that I would be there in three or four days and I would call when was just a few hours away. He promised to tell Mona.

I was getting close.

Chapter Fifty-three

Up, up and Away

Due to all the driving I had done in an incredibly short space of time I had become a tad impatient with my self-imposed lot in life. When I was ready to get off the road for the night.....I was ready that instant. I wanted the exit ramp to be a short one and to end at the campground gate or even better at the campground office.

The following day after a couple of hundred miles I arrived in Cloverdale. The campground listed in my book seemed reasonably priced with a few amenities like a swimming pool and an exchange library. I followed the signs and discovered after six or seven miles that the campground was nowhere in sight, not even a dot on the horizon. It was sheer torture. I still had no idea how far it was since I had run out of signs awhile back and wondered if I had missed a turn somewhere along the way. I kept driving anyway. I was just about to give up, turn around and head back to the highway when the sign said "just around the next bend and it'll be worth it." Well, just around the next bend was a seven-percent grade up to the heavens and then a dirt road. My van was wheezing because of the altitude and I was wheezing and snorting because of the aggravation that this damn campground had already put me through and I wasn't there yet.

The campground had changed ownership. The spot was eight dollars more than listed in the book. The price of admission was twenty-six dollars and seventy-five cents and believe me "it wasn't worth it." Owen and Betty Bennett from British Columbia were in line ahead of me at the cash and they, too, were upset with the distance and the high-falutin price tag. We decided that it was too far back to the highway and since we had failed to drop bread crumbs on route we would not find our way back easily. We grudgingly paid for one night of camping.

We were parked side by side and over whiskey and coke we discussed the outrageous prices, some of the more exotic foods we enjoyed and places in the world that we loved. By the time we finished the second drink in the series of I don't know how many, we were nice and relaxed, not having a care in the world. We enjoyed hamburgers and hot dogs on the barbecue, a bottle of red wine that I brought to the picnic and when it got dark and little things started biting we packed it in for the night. I fell asleep quickly, slept well and awoke early without a hangover.

I wasn't long on the highway when I found the first mileage sign. I was approximately one hundred miles north of San Francisco. I drove straight through, not even stopping for a brief look. What a waste! I was, however, finding camping in California rather expensive. I'm sure it would have been much cheaper by the week or month but daily it was not affordable.

Despite the fact that I didn't stop much, I was thoroughly enjoying the Oregon and California coastline. It was very reminiscent of the Algarve in Portugal with the massive rock formations jutting out of the water. That night I camped in the Big Sur area of the Monterey Peninsula. I was happy to have electricity even though there was no television reception. It was dark early in the evening and I didn't want to run my battery down with the lighting nor did I want to sit in the dark.

In my wandering around the campground I ended up talking with two French women. One, the mother of two children, was involved in a most interesting and tragic predicament. Pierrette had come to live in California with her husband and family. Within a few years her husband left her for another woman. A custody battle ensued. They both won and shared custody of an eight-year-old girl and a six-year-old boy. She could not find a job because of her lack of language skills. He was not generous with support payments. She was not happy in California and wanted to return to her home in France. She would have to leave her children behind. "The situation" she said "is unthinkable. I cannot leave my children."

"I say shoot the bastard. This is California," I said, "a jury will understand."

We all laughed but the twinkle in her eyes made me wonder if she thought I was serious. We shared our stories and the wine until the evening chill sent us indoors. I spent the rest of the night playing computer games.

I arrived in Beullton early the next day. I was within easy reach of Mona, had she been home. I spent the afternoon walking around the town. I had a bowl of the finest that Pea Soup Anderson's had to offer. I found a couple of antique stores, or to be more truthful junk shops, and went through them. I had been to Beullton on several other occasions, once with my husband, so the place brought back a lot of memories. I didn't mind wandering the few back streets just for some exercise but found little of interest.

I returned to the campground and spent a couple of hours reading, some time swimming and at least an hour in the hot tub. It was soothing and warm and rejuvenating. I tried calling Mona every hour on the hour. I finally managed to reach her a little after eleven that night. We talked for a while. She promised she would stay home the next day and wait for my call. I was about three hours from Chatsworth. I would see her the next day.

I rested easy that night.

Chapter Fifty-four

Geriatric Thelma and Louise

I called her from a service station pay phone as soon as I got off the highway at the exit she had given me the night before. I needed exact directions. I didn't want to be roaming around or heading the wrong way on any particular street, certainly not in a city this size and so close to Los Angeles. Her directions were perfect and I had no problem maneuvering the side streets. I was waiting in the strip mall parking lot when Mona pulled up with her son David in his jeep. After a few quick hugs and kisses David drove back to the condo alone and Mona rode with me.

I was too late to sit on the furniture. Much of it had been sold because the apartment they were moving into was much smaller. Mona seemed happy to be getting a fresh start even though the new apartment was close to the old one and she still had no idea what she would be doing for a job.

My sister has a tremendous amount of energy. We were on the go from the minute I arrived to the minute she packed a small suitcase and took off with me into the great unknown.

Every day after packing a few boxes we met her friends for coffee and conversation at a local donut shop. Depending on their circumstances different friends arrived on different days and at different times. Some were working. Some were coming in only for lunch. Some were waiting for their "big break." Some were forever unemployed. There was definitely an assortment.....and I'm not just talking donuts here.

The topics of conversation were as varied as the participants with Mona asking the questions or leading the pack with what's going on, the crime rate, the unemployment rate, where they were going to build the new prison, where to go roller blading and bicycle riding or what's happening in Santa Monica, a favorite spot of hers.

We drove down to Santa Monica one afternoon so she could roller blade in the park. Not being quite so brave, never having done it before, I watched and had no desire to join in after seeing her put on her wristbands, elbow pads and kneepads and finally her helmet. I loved watching her skate around and so did others. They didn't often see gray-haired ladies enjoying their sport so many stopped and waved and wanted to talk when she was through.

Before checking out the craft shops, the antique shops and the bookstores we had lunch in a restaurant overlooking the water. The day just went.

One evening we met her son Michael and a new girlfriend for dinner at the Santa Monica pier. I don't think I would have recognized him. He was so handsome. I felt he should be in front of the camera instead of moving all the heavy equipment around as a grip for the movie industry. He loved what he was doing.

I spent another afternoon with David watching all the funny videos he had made or seeing the bit parts he had been involved in on television. He was in a commercial for The Dating Game. He was standing behind Jay Leno while Jay was doing his street interviews. He was a contestant on several game shows. David stuck his gorgeous face with dazzling green eyes like his mother's in front of every camera he came across.

I had been in Los Angeles almost a week and was getting anxious to be on my way. I wanted an oil and filter change for the van before getting back on the road. The van was moved from the garage area in the alley behind Mona's apartment to back onto the street. I called a VW dealer for service and was given an appointment for early that afternoon. I hadn't used it much since my arrival.

The van wouldn't start. The Auto Club boosted the battery and I drove it to the service station where it stayed overnight. I paid the one hundred fifty-seven dollars for an oil change, a couple of hoses and a battery boost. He said everything else was okay and I shouldn't have any more problems. It seems that the refrigerator had been running off the battery and ran it down. That was all.

The next day was our last at her old apartment and we had lots to do. Some of her treasures that she couldn't part with but wouldn't fit into her apartment went into a storage unit. We moved some boxes to her new place. We did a room-by-room cleaning of her old apartment even though the date had been set for the complex to be demolished. We packed my van and I followed her back to storage where she would leave her car.

By the time we were road-ready it was almost two-thirty in the afternoon and I was exhausted. I suggested that we stay close by until the next day but she was anxious to be on the road. I told her that I liked to be off the road by four-thirty but that didn't deter Mona. She insisted that we head out. She didn't want to spend another night in Los Angeles. So there we were, geriatric Thelma and Louise, hittin' the road.

Chapter Fifty-five

Junk

Right around the time that I like my drive day to end, sometimes more urgently than at other times, we were in Barstow, California. The few campgrounds that we saw were located right off the main street and all looked the same with old, dilapidated, rust-bucket trailers that hadn't moved since the flood. Neither one of us wanted to stay but I was tired, getting irritable and wanted to be off the road. Mona insisted that we could make it to Stateline, Nevada before dark. Against my better judgment, and not knowing what else to do, we moved on. We gassed up and picked up a couple of sandwiches before getting back on the highway.

We were on the Baker Grade when it happened. It was a straight road but a long steady incline. I was just trying to pass a slow moving truck when the van spluttered. Our heart's spluttered with it. It didn't die but it sure felt like it wanted to. After an "Oh my God, what was that!" from both of us we fell silent. My mouth went as dry as if I had been sucking a day-old wine stain out of a shag carpet and my heart started pounding. In that brief instant I felt I was going to be sick.

"Pull over and stop," Mona said trying desperately to control the quiver in her voice.

I said nothing. I wanted to shriek some obscenity at her for leaving so late and being on the road long after I felt confident.....but I said nothing. I just kept driving and praying. It was getting dark. We were both terrified of being stranded out in the desert with a useless vehicle, some food and water, but with no protection from the elements and no way of calling anyone for help.

It was over a hill that we saw the lights in the distance. "I hope it's Stateline and not just signs advertising Stateline," said Mona.

By the time we got a little closer we both realized that there was some kind of civilization out there. Not much but I didn't care. I just wanted to get there. Those lights were a lot farther than they seemed.

We made it. I breathed a long sigh of relief when I parked in front of the office. I told Mona to stay with the van because I knew that if I shut the damn thing off I wouldn't be able to get it going again. I returned with a paid up spot for the night. I pulled into the first available spot, turned off the motor and pulled the key out. The van continued to run as if nothing had happened. I panicked.

I called over a neighbor who took his place behind the wheel of my van. He put it in gear and took his foot off the clutch. It jumped and died. So did my confidence. He started and stopped the van a couple of times.

"It all seems okay now," he said.

Las Vegas was about fifty miles away but we would worry about that the next day. We were safe.....at least for the moment.....at least for the night. We walked over to one of the casinos for dinner but I just couldn't eat anything.

The thought of getting back into the van and driving the next day did not have any appeal to me. I was a nervous wreck. My confidence was shot and I was sick to my stomach at even the thought of getting behind the wheel. We stayed in Stateline the next day.

We visited with our neighbor, John Barney and his dog, Joe. In the afternoon we went into all the gambling spots that we could walk to.....Whiskey Pete's, Buffalo Bill's and Primadonna's. They all seemed to have fun houses connected to the gambling casinos. Mona went on the Roller Coaster. We rode the Flume and we walked the casinos putting a few coins in the slots.

To lift my spirits I started thinking of alternative plans for The Puppy, like giving it a shot and putting it out of its misery or to be more precise, my misery. I considered sending the van back to Florida by transport or train. I considered selling the van in Las Vegas. I considered junking it if I couldn't sell it. I considered storing it in Las Vegas for a few months and returning when I was better able to deal with it. Driving it had taken more out of me than I cared to talk about. I hated it.

Since I hadn't slept well that night we got up early. Mona went out for breakfast while I cleaned the van putting everything away so it wouldn't rattle around. When she returned I sent her off with a large, red thermos to be filled with fresh drinking water and as much ice as would fit. I told her I would pick her up outside the hotel.

I was fully loaded. I was ready to go. I turned the key in the ignition. Nothing. I tried again. Nothing. I tried a third time. Nothing. I tried a fourth. A tiny spark. I tried again. God knows how but that one little spark caught. The van groaned and started.

I picked up Mona who was waiting with the water-and-ice filled thermos. If we were going to be stranded in the desert at least it would be in daylight and with enough water to bathe in.

We never turned off the motor. We drove straight to a VW dealer in Las Vegas. They said they would look at it later that day but would guarantee nothing. It was a Canadian van with Canadian specifications and they would not give me any assurances.

I told them I would bring it back after we found a place to stay. We found a hotel room at the Hacienda. We unloaded the van. I took off the bicycle and the rack and delivered it back to the dealer. I knew that when I got through with the repairs my money would be gone. I figured it would run into the thousands.

I really didn't care at this point because I was ready to give up the van, the trip and my resolve. They could offer me any price for it and I would have taken it.

Chapter Fifty-six

More Problems

We took our time getting back to the room. The service manager had told me that it would be at least until noon the next day before anyone could take a look at it so we didn't rush. It was after six when we walked in and saw the message light blinking on the phone. The message was from the manager at the dealership and I was to call him back as soon as possible. I called. The service department was closed.

My mind shifted immediately into overdrive. Did they not want to work on a Canadian van? Did they not have the parts? Would it take a month to get the parts? I pushed it all to the back of my mind knowing that I could keep it well buried until about two o'clock in the morning. At least I didn't have to drive it anymore that day. I would deal with whatever happened the next day.

The next day came very early, much earlier than I would have considered calling. The manager was on the other end of the phone at seven-thirty. The best news would have been that the van had mysteriously burned up during the night, was not repairable and my insurance would cover buying me a new one off the showroom floor but that didn't happen. The second best news was okay too.

ALASKA BOUND *and Gagged*

It seems that the mechanic knew exactly what the problem was. Several others with the exact same problem had come in within the last few days. The transformer had gone out and would have to be replaced. The electrical portion of the ignition switch had malfunctioned and had to be replaced as well. Two cells in the battery had been damaged, which was understandable since the battery was already almost a month old. (It had been replaced in Prince Rupert, British Columbia) All would be taken care of by noon that day and would cost approximately four hundred dollars.

"Go for it," I said. Actually what else could I say? There was nowhere else within a thousand-mile radius I could have taken it to, even if it did run properly.

The three days that Mona and I spent in Las Vegas were fabulous, dahling, absolutely fabulous. I had not been there in twenty-five years and the changes were monumental. The hotels were numerous and architectural works of art. The interiors were awesome.

"Why do you want to go to Egypt?" Mona asked. "Just spend a couple of days at the Luxor. No difference! Why go to Italy when a couple of days at Caesar's Palace would be the Coliseum without the jet lag. Spend a couple of days at the MGM, in the shape of a lion's head, and you'll feel like you're in the Wizard of Oz. The Mirage has a jungle theme with live leopards living behind glass walls. So who needs Africa?" she said.

We walked from hotel to hotel. One of them had a volcano erupting every fifteen minutes after dark and another had pirates fighting from well-manned frigates every hour on the half hour.

The life in Las Vegas was a world away from Alaska. Despite the hundred degree temperatures it didn't prevent us from doing a little street dancing. Line dance lessons were included. The music blasted out onto the patio.

I loved the time we spent in Las Vegas. We relaxed around the pool in the afternoon and played board games with some of the other guests. From a city bus we did some sightseeing, getting on and off when we felt like it.

Mona called a friend or two in the real estate business but there was nothing available for her job-wise. As much as I hated to think about it, it was time to move on. The day we left was very, very windy but the van handled it well. We had absolutely no problem.

We stopped in Mesquite so that we could see the new casino built by Merv Griffin for forty-five million dollars. The joke of the time was that Merv and the Devil were fighting over property. The Devil won and took Hell. Merv got Mesquite. For a true gambler the casino was perfect. There was nothing else around.

We had no trouble making it to St. George, Utah. We spent a couple of hours walking the mall. I had some pictures developed. We had dinner at a Shoney's that was walking distance to the campground. It all felt good and familiar for a change. When we got back to the campground I discovered that my refrigerator was not working. I decided to wait until I got back to Toronto before I had it fixed. Mona seemed to prefer eating out anyway and I didn't want to be in the middle of nowhere (again) when I had more repairs done.

We had a great day in St. George. We visited the Latter Day Saints Church, the Daughters of Utah Pioneer Museum and Brigham Young's winter home. We walked from one end of town to the other and stopped for coffee and pastry on route. We had dinner at Kenny Roger's Restaurant with another walk through town. We spent the evening in the television room of the campground doing puzzles.

ALASKA BOUND *and Gagged*

It will probably be the end of the book or perhaps the end of my life before I stop saying how relieved I was every day that the van drove well and without something else going tilt. Since the refrigerator didn't hinder my getting from place to place I didn't give it too much thought.

We had breakfast at Shoney's, picked up some fruit at the market in St. George and before entering Zion National Park we saw the Cinemax Movie (IMAX) that was filmed in Zion. This was my first. It was on a three-story high screen and every inch jumped out in infinite detail.

We stopped at the visitor's center to pick up a walking map of some of the trails. We chose a spot for a one-hour walk. Before we got too far up the trail, we were forced to wait for the rangers who were bringing someone down on a stretcher. The walkway was very narrow. We knew we had to be careful. It would not do to have either one of us incapacitated. The walked was strenuous but just what we needed to get the kinks out. We marveled at the deep crevasses that were cut into the landscape.

Back at the van we drove slowly through the park thoroughly enjoying the scenery before leaving via the east side of Zion.

It was an easy drive to Kanab, which has been used in the movies since the forties. The earth is bright red clay and as you enter the town the sign says, "Welcome to Kanab, the Greatest Earth of Show."

We found a wonderful place to camp. It was very small, very clean and very friendly. Mona enjoyed a bike ride while I treated myself to a chat with the neighbors and the campground owners and hosts.

Besides with only one bike we were not too likely to go tandem. The evening was pleasant enough. We relaxed over a spaghetti dinner at a local restaurant and then a walk through town to check out the other campgrounds to make sure that we had made the right decision. We went out for ice cream. My good times were very short-lived. That was my last evening of peace.

Chapter Fifty-seven

The Problems Continue

Since my condo in Florida had been rented the many months that I had been away and I had been depositing the rent checks monthly I did not anticipate any problems when I called the bank to see if the check had cleared like all the months before. This time, however, I received an unpleasant surprise. The check had been returned Non Sufficient Funds. I called the condo several times only to have the phone picked up by the answering machine. I wasn't too concerned at the time. I assumed that it was an oversight. My gut just tied itself into the tiniest little bow of uncertainty. Mona and I had cereal for breakfast and left the campground.

The drive through the Painted Desert was beautiful but long. Having had so much van trouble I did not feel comfortable with all of the open spaces and since time was running short we decided to skip the Grand Canyon. We would save it for another excursion.

While strolling through St. George we stopped at a travel agency and Mona had purchased a plane ticket for home. We had been on the road about ten days and she was getting a little antsy. She would be returning to Los Angeles from Albuquerque. Had we stopped in the Grand Canyon we would have had to rush through the park and then rush to meet the plane. Given our recent motorhoming history neither one of us felt comfortable about putting ourselves in that frantic mode. We bypassed what we knew was one of the most beautiful places on earth.

We stopped for a couple of hours at Lake Powell and the Dam. We were impressed. We drove straight through to Flagstaff, Arizona. We camped that night at Black Bart's Steakhouse and campground. The barbecued rib and chicken dinner was superb, the first I had enjoyed in a long while and we spent the evening listening to the singing waiters and waitresses.

When I couldn't reach the tenant at my condo that evening I called a mutual friend. Apparently it had not been an oversight. The air conditioner had gone out in my condo; the repair bill would have been over a thousand dollars so he moved out.

My decision was an easy one. After I took my sister to the plane in Albuquerque I would have to head directly and quickly to Florida. A home without an air conditioner in Florida soon becomes a jungle complete with moss hanging on the walls, fungus growing in your shoes, a velvety growth over the carpets and various sizes of moving things with four, six and eight or more legs.

I had no idea when the air conditioner had gone out and I certainly didn't want to dwell on what I would find. I just knew that I had to get there and fast. Mona's plane, however, was not until the twenty-eighth of September and it was only the twenty-fifth. Like it or not I would have to wait.

The next morning we headed out early. We stopped for breakfast and gas at a little roadside café about an hour on the road and stopped again at a shopping mall in Gallop, New Mexico for a short breather. The tension had returned with a vengeance. Lunch did not sound the least bit appealing. We had ice cream.

I loved having my sister with me but I had been on the road far too long. It had been five and a half months since I had left Florida. I was road weary and sick to death of all the problems that had plagued me on this trip. I knew that the problems would not be over even after I got to Florida. I was concerned about the state of my condo. It contained almost everything I owned especially the only pictures I had of my husband. I would be devastated if everything had gone to mildew.

We made our way to Albuquerque and beyond. I was tired of driving but we pushed on to Santa Fe. We looked for a campground upon our arrival and after a short visit to Santa Fe we discovered that the closest campground was another thirteen miles up the road. The last thirteen miles were endless.

I pulled in, stopped the van, turned off the motor and burst into tears.

"What's the matter?" Mona asked. "We're here. We're okay. What's the matter?" she asked again.

I just shook my head. I couldn't talk. She let me cry until I couldn't cry anymore.

Chapter Fifty-eight

Revisited

"What's the matter?" she asked, her emerald green eyes filling with tears as she looked at me.

"Paul and I stayed in this campground when we drove out west in 1991," I said still sniveling a little. "I recognized the little theater after we drove in."

"We don't have to stay here. There's another campground about five miles up the road," she said. "Why don't we go there?"

"No, I'll be okay in a minute," I said gasping for breath. "There are things I'll have to face alone for the rest of my life. I run from nothing. Not even this. Just give me another minute or two."

I dried my eyes while looking into the rear view mirror and took a couple of deep breaths. When I felt I looked reasonably presentable I went into the office to pay for a couple of nights. We found our spot and settled in. There were no restaurants in the area so dinner that night was a can of soup and a peanut butter and jelly sandwich. It tasted surprising good since we were both tired and hungry. That night in the little movie theater we watched Ace Ventura with Jim Carrey. It was just stupid enough to be really funny.

ALASKA BOUND *and Gagged*

We drove into Santa Fe early the next morning. We headed for a coffee shop for breakfast, relaxed over a cup and left with an extra large Styrofoam cup of some exotic blend in hand. We wandered into every shop, museum and artist's gallery, sipping as we walked the crowded streets of the unique tourist area. We watched craftsmen at work and fingered every piece of wood and wrought iron we came across. When we sat on a park bench looking at the colorful store windows we realized that every second story balcony had strings of hot red peppers hanging from the rafters.

The local native people had a street sale at the open-air market. We wandered from booth to booth checking out the woven shawls, scarves and blankets, the hand crafted jewelry and the hand painted skirts and blouses. It didn't seem to matter what we saw it all had a dash of turquoise in it. Seeing my favorite color seemed to lift my spirits. I purchased a pair of earrings with turquoise stones that matched my ring.

Before returning to the campground we found a supermarket, picked up a barbecued chicken and a bottle of wine. That night we watched Junior with Danny DeVito and Arnold Schwarzenegger. Again, stupid enough for a few good chuckles.

We left Santa Fe early the next morning. They were not calling for nice weather and since Mona's plane ticket was for eleven o'clock that night I thought we might be able to find a campground early in the afternoon and close to the airport. I thought we might spend the day touring Albuquerque enjoying the sights and perhaps take in a late movie before I took her to the airport. She wanted to go to the airport first and see if she could get on an earlier flight.

We did not get far before the rain started teeming down. My driving slowed considerably as the weather got worse. We still had to find the airport and couldn't see the street names.

Joei Carlton Hossack

The map I had was very good but it indicated an airport north of the city. We quickly ran out of airport signs so I decided to head for the airport south of the city. Mona became fidgety and as she started moving around I couldn't see out of the passenger side mirror, which lead me to shriek at her to sit still. Cars were whizzing past me on both sides and I needed her help to get into the slow lane just in case I had to pull off quickly.

"Sit back in your seat. I'll find the God damn place," I said a little quieter. "I need to be able to see out of that mirror," I reminded her. "It is the only view I have of that side of the van and of the cars coming up alongside.

As she was apologizing we started seeing airport signs again. We would be getting off the highway in a couple of miles. The rain had abated slightly but the streets were flooded.

At the airport I parked right in front of 'departures' and waited while Mona went inside. I hoped no one would come to shoo me away since the sign that hung over the door said, 'drop off passengers only'. Mona was taking longer than I expected. When she returned she said, "I need my luggage. There's a plane leaving in ten minutes and they're holding a seat." We had a fast hug and she was gone.

I was happy that we would not have to roam around a big city all day in the rain. I was also pleased that she would not be flying after midnight or waiting for hours in the wee hours of the morning at some shabby airport in the middle of nowhere. But all of a sudden my sister was gone. I was alone again. The heaviness was almost more than I could bear. I stayed rooted to the spot and just cried.

Since the windshield and side windows were all fogged up I decided to wait, with the motor running and heat blasting, and cry it out.

ALASKA BOUND *and Gagged*

It didn't take too long before I was back on the highway heading north. I found my exit and decided to drive east until I felt like spending the night. The rain continued, heavy at times, but I just kept driving through it. I was almost happy for the inclement weather. It forced me to think about the driving rather than missing my sister. I vowed that I would not let the years go by without spending lots of time with her.

With nothing else to do on the endless straight road I reviewed our lives. We had both been away from our Montreal home for more years than I cared to think about. She moved to California when she was eighteen. She married at nineteen. Five years later I moved to California at eighteen, but I was the "baby sister" and we did not see or speak to each other often. We became friends when I was twenty-three and by that time she had two rambunctious boys, David and Michael. I was busy leading the life of a single, working-two-jobs, gal of the sixties. When Mona's children were a little older I moved back to Canada while she moved to Texas. I got married and settled down. I guess that this was the way things were supposed to be. We stayed in touch with letters or by phone occasionally. Mona would visit Montreal and see our father and our two brothers.

But the years had brought about many changes. Mona was back in California. I was widowed. Our father had died so her visits to Montreal were rare. I vowed again that I would not let years go by without seeing her. I liked being one of the 'geriatric Thelma and Louise' a name given to us by our older brother. This trip had been the longest time together since we were children. There had been some tense moments but I had loved every minute of being with her. I missed her.

I drove almost non-stop to Tucumcari, New Mexico. The rain came down in sheets and the windshield wipers had trouble keeping up. In the last few miles of driving the gusts of wind had picked up considerably and was swatting the van from one side of the lane to the other like a ping pong player in rare form. I found a campground near the highway and stopped around four o'clock. I was glad to be off the road. I was exhausted and there had been tornado warnings for Amarillo, Texas. At that point, the way the trip had been going so far, Amarillo was much too close for comfort.

For the next four days I drove and drove and drove. I averaged about four hundred and fifty miles per day. I stayed in Bowie, Texas one night. I camped in Rayville, Louisiana another night and a wonderful campground in Troy, Alabama a third night. On the fourth night I arrived in Sarasota, Florida.

I wish I could say that this was the end of the story, however what I walked into was a disaster. My six months on the road were no where near over.

Chapter Fifty-nine

If Looks Could Kill

That night I arranged to stay with my neighbor Sadie Karsh. Her second bedroom had a comfortable rollaway single bed and the bedroom window looked out at my condo directly across on the dead end street.

I don't know how long the air conditioner had been off but for the short time that I was in there it felt like I could slow-roast a rack of ribs. All the fans were circulating on low, which did absolutely nothing. It was stifling. The air was musty and not breathable for anyone other than a natural-born Floridian.

I really didn't have a chance to get a good look around. Even though my tenant had stopped payment on the rent and he himself had physically moved out, he had left everything he owned, and then some, in my condo. I couldn't even turn around without bumping into something that didn't belong to me.

The following morning, when I made a thorough inspection, I discovered what he had done. The condo had been rented furnished. I had mentioned that if he had any spare pieces of furniture they could be left on the lanai (Florida room) because it was empty. Although the condo had two bedrooms I had rented it as a one bedroom with my personal belongings left in the back bedroom.

Joei Carlton Hossack

He had agreed to it at the time. It obviously did not suit his needs once he had the lease and had moved in. He moved my furniture onto the lanai and his took their place. His clothes and personal effects were filled to the brim in every closet including the large walk-in closet in the back bedroom. Every personal item I had left in the back room had been moved into the lanai. I was so angry I wanted to scream. The feeling passed.

I was whipped. I wanted to cry. I went back to Sadie's. I called an air conditioning company. They came that day to give me an estimate.

The news was all bad. The compressor had gone out and would cost a little over a thousand dollars to replace. The air conditioner was over ten years old and they did not recommend putting a new compressor on a ten-year-old machine. They recommended a new air conditioning system that along with the rebate from the government would cost two thousand eight hundred dollars. I had no choice. I signed on the dotted line. I was not a happy camper.

In searching the house I found a business telephone number for my tenant. Before calling him I called the telephone company and discovered that there was a ninety dollar outstanding bill on my phone. I called Florida Light and Power and learned that ninety-three dollars was owed. Since my FLP bills had never run over forty dollars I suspected that they were long, long overdue.

In a moment of fury and under the incorrect assumption (advice given to me by a knowledgeable friend) that once the tenant stops paying rent the rental agreement is null and void, I had the locks changed on the condo. BAD MISTAKE on my part. I then called the tenant and told him to pay the bills or he would not get his stuff back.

ALASKA BOUND *and Gagged*

That afternoon the outside portion of the air conditioner was changed and I arranged for the electrical work to be done on that Friday. I visited friends that evening and returned home to discover that my tenant had changed the locks. I called the police.

I learned that I was totally in the wrong for changing the locks in the first place. According to the law once a tenant has a lease, whether the rent is paid or not, whether the house is like a pigsty or not, whether utilities are paid or not, THE LANDLORD HAS NO RIGHTS.

I stayed with Sadie that night. She assured me I could stay as long as necessary. The tenant would not let anyone in to finish the electrical portion of the air conditioning system. I sat at Sadie's house and watched the action of his packing and not doing much else. I ate my guts out. Several days went by and I thought I would go mad. I didn't want to see any of my friends since I would have to explain my plight and my stupidity.

Since I still had business to take care of in Canada, my friend Vivian urged me to leave before I went berserk and did something equally as stupid as changing the locks or changing his face.

Vivian offered her help and would call me in Canada when the condo was empty. She would do the inspection with the police department and then have the locks changed for the umpteenth time. Since changing the locks had been her suggestion in the first place she had felt partially responsible. I was grateful for her help.

I left my Westphalia van with a friend. I had my Ford Escort serviced at the dealer. With just a few articles of clothing, my toiletries and my credit cards I left around noon.

Chapter Sixty

Ships That Pass in the Night

Except to stop for gas I drove non-stop to Valdosta, Georgia. Driving my well-tuned up car usually relaxed me and to a tiny degree this was no exception but I was not feeling good. I felt displaced, despondent and homeless. I would have to fight to get my home back. "Why had I rented it in the first place?" I scolded myself. He was a friend of a friend, newly divorced and needed a place to stay. I was leaving anyway. These four elements combined would prove to be my downfall. Of this I felt sure.

My choice for a motel room that night was a poor one. The room was nice enough but it was well back in the motel lot and there were not many people around. I was feeling jittery and needed a long walk in the fresh air to clear my head. I didn't feel like driving to go out to dinner but I especially didn't want the long walk beside all the empty motel rooms after dark so I drove.

Dinner was not pleasant either. There were just a few people in the restaurant and most looked like they had just gotten off work. There were no older couples and no single women dining alone. I ordered the deep-fried shrimp platter hoping it would entice my palate to send forth a taste bud or two. It didn't. I nibbled on a couple of shrimp and a french fry or two and took the rest back to the room hoping I could finish the meal watching television. That seemed to work a little better. I spent the rest of the night watching television. Just before bed I took a long, slow bath. I slept fitfully but I slept. I was exhausted.

The next day was another long, uneventful, mind numbing drive day. I stopped twenty miles south of Lexington, Kentucky and this time made a better choice of hotel. I took an hour or so to rest and then another hour in a hot bath before changing my clothes for dinner. Dinner at the Cracker Barrel restaurant was right across the parking lot and by the time I made my entrance it was crowded. I always enjoyed people watching.

I left my name and the number in my party with the hostess. There were many people waiting and the older gentleman ahead of me was alone as well. After I left my name there were several people behind me in line waiting to leave their names. I browsed through the well-stocked shop connected to the restaurant. I picked up a T-shirt or two to check the picture on the front. I smelled some of the handmade soaps. I turned the keys on a couple of music boxes and listened to the tunes. I sniffed the scented candles.

The longer I waited the less hungry I became. The relaxing bath had worn off and I was becoming agitated again, my stomach tying in a knot. I was longing for someone to talk to and went back to check the list to see if perhaps another lady had come in alone.

Perhaps the people on the list after me said they wanted smoking but both the name ahead of mine and mine were skipped over. Out of the corner of my eye I saw the man approaching. I screwed up my courage and said quickly, "we both seem to be dining alone in the non-smoking section. Would you care to share a table?"

Joei Carlton Hossack

The change in his face was dramatic and immediate. His eyes opened wide and glowed. He gave me a big smile and said, "now that would be wonderful." He was obviously as thrilled with the prospect of a dinner companion as I was and we were chatting even before we arrived at our table, which they showed us to immediately.

"I'm heading south," he said. "I was visiting my children and grandchildren in Toledo for a few days. I miss them and it's so far from Atlanta. I only see them a couple of times a year."

"I spend my winter in Florida," I confided, "but my family live in Toronto and Montreal. I miss them also but I spend six months of the year traveling. I have a condo in Sarasota."

"We live in a senior residence in Atlanta," he volunteered.

"We?" I asked. "Your wife doesn't drive with you to see your children?"

"No," he replied, a touch of sadness in his voice. "She has Alzheimer's and doesn't recognize anyone anymore.

"I'm so sorry. It must be a terrible disease to have to deal with. How long have you been married?" I asked.

"Fifty-one years."

"That's how old I am," I answered. "Fifty-one years. A lot can happen in fifty-one years. I have been widowed for three of those years."

"I'm sorry," he said. "I know that I shouldn't be telling you this but I now have a lady friend. I cannot tell my daughter. She just wouldn't understand."

"I know it's lonely," I said, "and you have to take the joy where you can find it. I'll find it again someday. I know I will."

"I know you will. You are a very pretty lady. Where did you travel to this year," he asked, opening an entirely new direction to our conversation.

"I drove to Alaska. I cannot believe how much driving I will have done by the time I get back to my home in Sarasota. If I get my home back," I said almost under my breath.

There was never a lull in the conversation and we were at least halfway through the meal before we introduced ourselves and admitted out loud how wonderful it was to have company. For the first time in I don't know how many days I relaxed enough to enjoy my meal. We even enjoyed dessert and a refill on the decaf coffee.

We said goodnight and goodbye in the parking lot. We shook both hands and wished each other a safe journey. The hour of sharing had changed my mood, my outlook, my entire day, in fact.

Chapter Sixty-one

The End of the Road

The following day was another long drive day with numerous construction lane restrictions and some road closures due to accidents. I didn't make it to my friend's house until close to eight o'clock and dark. Eva and Sam were having a dinner party with their family and without a moment's hesitation another place was set at the dinner table.

For the first time in a long time I felt safe. I was amongst friends. It didn't take me long to blurt out the story of my Florida problems but, once out in the open, I was able to set them aside temporarily.

Over the past six months I had not spent much time in a house that didn't shimmy on dirt roads or sway in the wind. I had not been with long-time friends who understood my lifestyle and I had been through a few too many trials and tribulations for my liking. For the moment I was safe. For the moment I felt an enormous amount of relief.

I tried to just enjoy the pleasure of being with people I knew, who wished me only health, wealth and happiness and the comforts of a real home. I busied myself with banking, a doctor's appointment, a dentist appointment and visiting other friends. Every once in a while my guts told me that I would have to start eviction proceedings and that I would again be living in a motorhome that never met a mechanic that it didn't want to have a long-term love affair with. I knew that I could not impose myself on my neighbor Sadie for the months that it would take to evict the tenant.

I vowed that I would never do this again. Just about the time I had convinced myself that it wouldn't be too bad living in a motorhome I got a call from Vivian in Florida telling me the tenant was out.

"Are you sure?" I said a little louder than I meant to.

"Yes, I went through the place with the police this morning. He's out," she said.

I wanted to cry. I wanted to scream. Eva got in the way and I hugged her a bit too hard. I had a home. I thanked Vivian and got off the phone.

After a week in Toronto I drove to Montreal to be with family and friends. I stayed only a few days. I was excited and edgy at the same time. I needed my home. I needed to put my feet up on furniture that belonged to me. I needed to get back to the normal life of someone who had a place to live.

On the way south I stopped in New Jersey for a night with my friends Amy and Norman Prestup. I normally stayed two days but after just one I was getting anxious and wanted to be on my way. Besides they were calling for a storm in the next day or two and I wanted to be farther south when it hit. My friends understood.

I left the next morning in sunshine. I was just south of Washington, D.C. when the rain started and the traffic slowed to a crawl. I inched my way homeward. I was not able to find a place to stay until Fredericksburg and there was so much traffic trying to get off the highway that it took over an hour to reach the exit. I pulled into the first hotel and thankfully they had a room on the second floor available.

Joei Carlton Hossack

At the end of each day heading south I felt a nagging niggle of relief. I took a short nap and a long, hot bath. I put on jeans and a sweatshirt to go out to dinner. In the doorway I met an older man traveling alone and we joined forces for dinner. I was getting good at this. By the time I returned to my room, flipped on the television set, took another hot bath to warm myself up I was ready for bed. I slept soundly.

By the time I arrived in northern Florida and found a room the tension had returned. I was glad to be getting home but I still had no idea what I would find once I got there. Vivian said my condo was okay but until I walked into it myself and knew that I was home, I would be uptight.

Vivian had been right. The condo was okay. Not as clean as I would have liked it and several items were missing, never to be located. But it was home. It felt relatively good. Once I changed the locks it felt even better.

I had my home back and for several days I couldn't bear to leave it. I couldn't drive. I told my friends that if they wanted to see me they would have to come get me. I didn't want to get behind the wheel of my car or my van. I had the feeling that I would get killed if I did. One day a short time later I drove the half-mile to the supermarket. Eventually I ventured a little farther.

In the six-and-a-half months of my adventure I drove close to twenty-five thousand miles. Much of that time I was alone. Had I driven in a straight line I would have driven around the earth at the equator. I returned a different person.

But I returned.

Epilogue

I had been back in Florida about a week when a message was left on my answering machine by my dear friend, Bud Albro. "Our tenant refuses to leave our house. We're homeless. Can we come stay with you?" A telephone number was left.

My friends had rented their beach house for the summer and now the tenant was refusing to leave. I called to say, "of course you can stay with me."

They stayed about a week. I loved having the company and they could have stayed as long as they wanted but once the tenant had been ousted they were anxious to get back to their home. I knew exactly how they felt.

We decided that there really are no homeless people in Sarasota. They are just people who have rented out their homes and their tenants have locked them out.

Landlord beware.

ABOUT THE AUTHOR:

Joei Carlton Hossack was born in February 1944 and raised in Montreal, Quebec, Canada. She has lived in Toronto, Canada, Los Angeles, California and Sarasota, Florida. She has spent most of the past thirteen years traveling the world gathering stories.

She is the author of Restless From The Start, Everyone's Dream Everyone's Nightmare, Kiss This Florida, I'm Outta Here and A Million Miles from Home. She is also a regular columnist for The Gypsy Journal.

She is currently a solo, full-time RVer and travels the United States and Canada writing, lecturing and entertaining.

Joei Carlton Hossack can be reached at: JoeiCarlton@Hotmail.com

A Million Miles from Home

Chapter One

The Sale

I watched as my small Renault Trafic motorhome went up the drive with a stranger behind the wheel. I had loved our little home on wheels and the freedom it represented. I had loved the exotic sights.....the London Bridge, the Tower of Pisa, the red-light district of Amsterdam, the Eiffel Tower, the Rock of Gibraltar, the Keurkehoff Gardens in full bloom. I reveled in the unusual sounds of traffic mixing with the shofar calling the devout to prayer or church bells heralding in Sunday morn or the town crier bringing news of the day. I loved listening to the many languages of the different countries and not having a clue as to what was being said. The smells.....sweet, pungent or something not to be identified until later, in all the numerous countries we had traveled through, brought back the most vivid of memories. The people that we had laughed with and shared a drink or meal with that we had met en route.....those memories opened the flood gate to tears. But mostly I had loved Paul, my traveling companion, my husband and lover of almost twenty years. That life was gone now. Only the memories lingered on to torture.

Paul, an investment dealer for Merrill, Lynch, and I, owner of a thriving wool business on the Danforth in Toronto's Greek/Italian section of town, had quit our jobs. We had sold our home in the Beach district. The boat, a twenty-four foot Grew, and both our vehicles went in the summer of 1989. For

1

ten years or more Paul had read every travel guide and studied every foreign map he could get his hands on. He had practiced good morning, good evening and how to order a beer in every country in Europe. He dreamt of just packing it all in one day and going. Being somewhat skeptical, I would believe that when I saw it. My skepticism never stopped him from planning and dreaming.

We left on the sixteen of September 1989. On the plane we just stared at each other. Were our friends right.....were we nuts?

In Britain we purchased a gently used 1987 beige and brown conversion van-style motorhome. The Renault Trafic was a very popular vehicle that year. Our two-and-a-half years on the road were filled with learning, excitement and a fair bit of danger. That second year we had traveled from Britain through Europe and were settled comfortably on the Greek Island of Crete when all hell broke loose. Our original plans were to tour the island, spending time in all the major cities and camping in Agio Galini. We were able to accomplish that bit of fun without too many problems or interference. From Crete we would be sailing to Rhodes. We planned on spending a week or two on Rhodes, hopefully finding a safe haven to store our motorhome. Paul and I would then sail the high seas or fly to Egypt to tour the ancient world before returning to reclaim our motorhome. We would then put our camper on the ferry and head for Turkey, our ultimate destination. The Gulf War put an end to those plans.

We stayed on Crete for several days hoping the Americans would put an end to the war quickly and we could continue our journey. We took it as a personal affront when they didn't do it. The refueling station of Hania, located on the north side of the island, was our downfall. Within three days they declared Crete a war zone and started issuing gas masks.

A Million Miles From Home

We were fairly confident that as tourists we were not going to be issued that precious commodity. With hordes of others and with great difficulty, we returned to the Greek mainland, sailed to Brindisi, Italy and a steady seven day drive took us to the south of Spain for a second winter.

While the 1991 Gulf War was a global tragedy, 1992 was a personal tragedy. Sixteen days into what was to have been a four-and-a-half month tour of visiting countries that had been behind the Iron Curtain when our travels started, my beautiful, fifty-two year old husband Paul had a heart attack while jogging and died in a stranger's car on the way to the hospital. We were in Germany at the time. We were on our way, for the second time, to Turkey.

The year after my Paul died I returned to England. I learned to drive the motorhome because selling the home we had loved so much was more than I could bear. I camped alone in it. I spent that summer working on three archaeological digs in the south, two in Kent County and one just outside of Norwich on an old Roman road. This was something that Paul and I had discussed and planned on doing together. I fulfilled our dream.

The van had been a perfect size for our gypsy way of life and the exorbitant price of gas. Camping alone in the van was a daily torture that I inflicted upon myself. It was much to small for me and my memories. When the archaeological digs were over I had not allowed myself enough time to sell the camper. I returned it to storage at the Barry Docks just south of Cardiff, Wales and returned to Canada, to family and friends, and then to Florida.

I returned to Wales in late May of the following year and, while staying with friends in Llancarfan, advertised the camper for sale in a motorhome magazine. While June sixth 1944 was D-Day for the world, June sixth 1994 was D-Day for

3

me. That was the day I closed that chapter in my life and watched as the motorhome went up the drive. Tears obstructed much of my view. I never saw it turn the corner out of the driveway.

It was a new life for both of us. I was disappointed that the camper had not been sold to another couple who would love the adventurous life as much as Paul and I had. It was an older gentleman who bought it and planned on using it to take his mother out on day trips. He could make her a cup of tea without having to go outside, he had told me. The camper would stay home while I would spread my wings and fly, perhaps even soar. I just prayed that I wouldn't crash land.

It was still early June and come hell, which I had already been through, and high water I was going to Turkey.....probably alone. It didn't take long to pack my belongings, since much of it had not been unpacked, and say good-bye to my friend Jan, whose Welsh-style long house I was staying in. The house, which stood on several acres of farmland on a small country road, was walking distance to a great eating pub in Llancarfan but about ten miles outside the hub of Cardiff. On a warm, sunny morning Jan drove me to the train station in Cardiff.

My first stop was to descend upon my friends in Temple Cloud, about twelve miles south of Bristol, England. I needed to prepare myself mentally for the trip. Jean and Bill Higgs, whom Paul and I had met camping at the beach in Menton, France and Barb and Glynn Webb, whom I had met the previous year, thanks to Bill and Jean, had all been to Turkey on numerous occasions. Surely they would give me all the advice I needed. I desperately needed courage even if it belonged to someone else.

With my two overstuffed pieces of luggage strapped onto mini wheels and a knapsack slung over my shoulder I

A Million Miles From Home

boarded the train in Cardiff for the short, uneventful ride to Bristol. From the Bristol train station I took the bus to the main bus terminal. I was already resentful of the amount of luggage I was totting around. I paid my one pound ten fare on the bus going to Temple Cloud and settled down to wait for it to leave. I was surprised and delighted at the ease with which I had begun my solo adventure. Granted I was in relatively familiar territory and the people did speak the language, to a large degree, although I did have to pay close attention at times.

There were only a few passengers on the bus since it was early afternoon on a workday. When a woman stood hunched over at the bus door struggling with a baby carriage, several department store bags and a baby, I went to help.

"I'll take the packages," I said as she handed them up to me without looking my way. I put them in the luggage holding area at the front of the bus and went back to take the baby stroller that she had now folded into a manageable size. As she handed it to me she looked up for the first time.

"Joei, you're back," said Cally with a real sparkle in her voice. She was a friend of the two couples I had stayed with the previous year. We settled in side-by-side for the twelve-mile journey.

Running into a familiar face thousands of miles away from my home in North America was my first indication that I would be okay. It was a small step but I suddenly knew deep down in my heart that I was becoming worldly.